Countercultural
Youth
Ministry

Countercultural
Youth
Ministry

By Aaron M. Arrowood

WOODSONG
P U B L I S H I N G

Seymour, IN

Countercultural Youth Ministry
By Aaron M. Arrowood

2016

Scripture quotations are from the King James Version of the Bible unless otherwise identified.

Woodsong Publishing
7100 Persimmon Lake Drive
Seymour, Indiana 47274

www.woodsongpublishing.com
Cover design by Vision Graphics
Printed in the United States of America.
ISBN 978-0-9979146-0-3

Table of Contents

1 - Introduction

They're lazy, uncultured, crude, loud, and ungodly. But, it's okay, they're teenagers. Right?

Imagine with me for a moment that you are the average unchurched American trying to live the American Dream... It's six AM or maybe PM, depending on what shift you work. An alarm startles you half-awake. You put on your jeans and work shirt or suit and tie, and head out the door. For eight or ten hours you work hard, if success is your motivation. Or, you give the man as little as you can. When your shift is complete you make the commute back home, grabbing fast food on the way. You finally arrive at your castle, or cave, sink into the couch, gripping a beer or a cola in one hand and the remote in the other. You crank up the entertainment and drift away. Mass media tells you what to be afraid of this week. Modern programming fearlessly takes you beyond moral boundaries into the foggy unknown with promises of endless pleasures. Tomorrow you will do it all again and desperately stretch towards the weekend. The highly anticipated task of becoming intoxicated is approached with enthusiasm. Inebriation allows you to live with impunity in the now.

Suddenly, without warning, it's Monday morning. An alarm commences a hangover that will make today's work singularly miserable. You trudge forward, week by week, occasionally managing to spend less than you earn in order to save for your children's future.

You want to make sure your progeny has the opportunity to live the dream.

Speaking of your offspring, they are being babysat by media and educated by the federal government. No concerns there. While you're knocking back a few cold ones, your kids are taught to explore every aberrant and potentially devastating trend, while rejecting everything wholesome. "Bad is good" says Wreck-it-Ralph. Perversion, recklessness, and insanity are piped into their minds through all sorts of electronic devices. If all this seems a little discouraging, don't worry; they'll get a very trendy, movie-based sermon on Sunday that will ward off any residual conscience that might be nagging at them. In a world where hedonism reigns, conviction must be the greatest enemy. Stop fretting, after all, they are just teens. You can't expect much. And, the Titanic is going to sink anyway. It's bad and it's going to get worse. Even the Bible says that. There's nothing to be done. Sit back, relax, and enjoy the orchestra.

That is what you have to work with…. So why youth ministry?

Is it really possible that you can make a difference in the world I just described? I am convinced that you can. Throughout history, very few people challenge the norms of society. Whenever someone does, they stand out. Speaking of the first-century church, Theodore Roszak writes, "Hopelessly estranged by ethos and social class from the official culture, the primitive Christian community… could not but seem an absurdity to the Greco-Roman orthodoxy." However, "all revolutionary changes are unthinkable until they happen … and then they are understood to be inevitable."[1]

I reject the fatalist's declaration that American culture is forever lost in the tide of amorality. I refuse to cling to the safety of indifference while my children drift on the remaining shards of a shattered heritage. Few though they may be, there are shining examples through history of men and women who threw down the gauntlet to their generations. Moses confronted Pharaoh. Gideon provoked the followers of Baal. Paul faced down the Pharisees. We can look to Esther, Lincoln, Mandela, Paine, Schindler, Luther, and Christ Himself for inspiration.

At some point weren't they all idealists—striving against the inevitable—for the absurd? But history could not resist the flood of their passion or the power of their message. They "turned the world upside down" but is the debauched and foolish direction of our culture irreversible? Is the current condition of society, alone in history, impervious to the powers that shake the foundations of humankind? To accept *that* is absurd. Official cultures are not powers in themselves, but only the mosaic of the individuals of whom they are comprised. **Individuals**. The world is shaped, and has always been shaped, by individuals. Individuals no better or worse than you.

This world is desperate for leaders. Christ enjoined us to pray "that He would send forth laborers." "The harvest is plenteous." The world is in need of revival. Don't give up on it yet. The revolution may very well begin with you. There is a stirring in the youth of this nation, an unrest. There are those who are ready to embrace a cause even if it compels them to live counter to their culture. These twelve, and fourteen, and seventeen year old potential dissidents are just waiting on a leader who will articulate the vision to be counter-cultural. You are that leader.

---

[1]The Making of a Counter Culture: Reflections on the Technocratic Society and Its Youthful Opposition (Berkley, CA: University of California Press, 1969), 43.

2 - The Countercultural Premise

"Countercultural Youth Ministry" is not a dream; it is the result of fifteen years as a youth pastor. I have a much better perspective than I did at twenty-four years of age. I'm writing because God, and an amazing group of teens, have taught me that young people are underestimated. I'm not writing because I think I have all the answers. I seriously considered entitling this book, "Dead-End-Ideas," or "39 Things Not to Do:" one mistake for every year I've been alive. I'm standing on a mountain of my own mistakes, but there is perspective up here.

I pity the students that suffered through my first years in ministry. My worst fear is that some of them are lost because of my mistakes. I pray for mercy on those that have lost their way because of my ignorance. I'm taking the time here to record for you, in a short format, some of the hard lessons I've learned that have formed principles that, if applied, will benefit your students.

This book comes from my personal experience with a youth group from Seymour, Indiana. This is not a compilation of the already written works of others, although there are many great books out there that you should certainly read. I'm not sharing the opinions of the experts or the ultra successful. The tone of this book may tend toward the autobiographical or philosophical, and hopefully will always be very biblical. I'm not going to present a book of statistics about trending youth methods.   Admittedly, this book is the synthesis of my own experiences and consequent opinions.   There is no one-size-fits-all ministry plan; however, I'm confident that I will share some principles that are worth your time. I've lived by them. I was defeated before I knew they existed. I've seen them remain true as groups have come and gone. I've mourned when they proved accurate in the lives of those that have fallen away. I've rejoiced when they worked for the unlikely overcomer.   In writing this book, I'm hoping for an additional blessing from a life of youth ministry: that hundreds, or even thousands of committed youth workers, would find some benefit from the sum of my experiences.

I define our students as a Countercultural Youth Ministry. This ministry follows the pattern of successful social revolutions, but is uniquely spiritual. It's loving but confrontational, compelling, and alienating.   It's meek but strong, familial, demanding, convicting, empowering. It is Christ-like.

Pastor, Mark Driscoll, describes Jesus this way:

"He tells people to 'Quit your jobs and follow me.' And he tells a demon 'shut up...' He heals a leper and says, 'You shut up too.' Jesus picks a fight with Sunday school teachers. He's angry and grieved .... He rebukes the wind. He kills two thousand pigs. He offends people, but doesn't go to sensitivity training .... He says, 'You guys are a bunch of hypocrites.' [He] Goes on a rant. He spits on a handicapped guy and calls Peter 'Satan.'"[2]

It is this same Jesus that chokes back the bitter cup of the cross, digs into His soul and finds the words, "Father forgive them for they know not what they do." Yes! This is the Jesus I find in Scripture. This is the very Jesus that established the countercultural team of twelve that turned the world upside down. The teens that gather around this God must by course become a Counter-Cultural Youth Group. They're bold, frail, broken, spirited, confident, overwhelmed, aching, confused, athletic, artistic, brilliant, apathetic, slovenly, passionate, quiet, and screaming, but most of all they are changed. They're striving to be Christ-like. Jesus said, "... I came not to send peace, but a sword" (Matthew 10:34). Joshua proclaimed, "Choose you this day whom ye will serve" (Joshua 24:15). We celebrate diversity in race, talents, and personalities, but students cannot come to Christ and remain the same. He compels us to make life altering choices. Either "come out from among, them and be ye separate" (2 Corinthians 6:17), or "I never knew you: depart from me" (Matthew 7:23). Sometimes we have to "mortify (kill) the deeds of the body" (Romans 8:13). Christ's followers have always been strangers and aliens (Elijah, Jeremiah, Daniel, Stephen, John the Baptist, Paul). They were Counterculturalists. We cannot be anything less. In a world of hatred and bigotry, we love. In a world of aberrant pleasures, we deny the flesh. In a world of social media and obesity, we pray and fast. In a world of entertainment, we read the Bible.

We are against sin, but we are not defined by what we're "not." We're counter/different, but we're not measured by the distance between ourselves and the world. We are different because we are Christ-like. Difference is effect, not motive. We don't look at the world and say, "I want to be different than that." We look at Jesus and say, "I want to be like Him." Jesus was the greatest of the countercultural revolutionists, but not just because He was God; more so, He denied Himself and gave His life for the world. That is our measuring stick. We will never achieve perfection in this life, but we intend to die trying. We consider this our "reasonable service." An unintended result of Christ-likeness is an ever-increasing gap between our lifestyle and the culture that we live in. Therefore, we become countercultural. As much as Jesus challenged and offended people, He also promised that if He were lifted up [on the cross], He would "draw all men" (John 12:32). Our mission is not to be religious hermits. In striving to be like Jesus, we experience the drawing power of the Cross; it's healing and forgiveness in our church and community.

In the chapters ahead, all the names and circumstances I share, unless otherwise noted, have been changed to protect the innocent and guilty.

I hope you enjoy *Countercultural Youth Ministry*.

---

[2]Mark Driscoll, How Human Was Jesus, https://marshill.com/media/vintagejesus/how-human-was-jesus/ajax_transcript?lang=en

3 - Why Youth Ministry

Working with teenagers, aged twelve to eighteen, has had its high points and some lows. I've received some incredulous looks from contemporaries who abandoned youth work at a much more reasonable age (i.e. when they could still play ping-pong without pulling a hammy). I'm passionate about what I do for two reasons. First, teenagers have potential that many, especially themselves, don't recognize. Secondly, many face almost unbelievable challenges, but with direction and support, they can be incredibly strong.

Working with teens awakens a feeling I had as an eleven year old, standing in front of a gas can holding a box of matches: "This is going to be amazing!"

The untrained amateur may look at teens and see braces, pimples, and awkwardness. But, I see a potential conflagration (extensive fire).

Let me introduce you to some of the exceptional teens I've worked with.

> Jennifer - She's mature, responsible, and motherly. She's brilliant and easy to be with. I can't predict what any of our teens will be, but I wouldn't at all be surprised if she entered a medical career, or became a missionary.

Max - He's athletic, strong, and he thinks he's a ladies' man. He has the talent and the willingness to do anything for you.

Emma - She's a potentially award winning poet with flawless execution. Her poise at 13 leaves admirers in awe. She is truly a rare talent.

Adalyn - She's resourceful and tech-savvy. Give her a bucket of parts and she'll build you a computer. Ask her to use her own car to spend the day taking care of underprivileged children and she will thank you for allowing her to be a part.

Colton - His home life seems normal. He has an active father and a faithful, if distant, stepmom. He's intelligent and athletic. He's the guy everyone wants on the team no matter what sport you're playing. He's fashion conscious and always looks like success.

Julia - She's been an overcomer. She's been dealt a hard hand, but she has taken it in stride. She's a fighter.

There are many more I could mention. These teens are going to change the world. They will make wonderful husbands and wives, fathers and mothers. They will impact universities and marketplaces. They will be community leaders and church pillars. They will be Sunday School teachers, prayer warriors, pastors, missionaries, and soul winners. I count it a privilege beyond my station to have the chance to work with them at this critical stage in their lives.

Then there is the second reason I feel compelled to work with teens. Behind the smiles, the laughter, and the potential are hurts and challenges that defy reason. Let me share what Paul Harvey would have called, "The Rest of the Story." Here is the same list of teens:

Jennifer, along with her father and sister, found out through the grapevine that her mother was involved with prostitution. Shortly thereafter, her mother passed away at a very young age. Jennifer is still trying to deal with the shame and a new stepmom.

When Max was 8 years old, doctors diagnosed his father with a lethal heart condition. He would die in less than a year. Max, estranged from his father, never got to say goodbye.

Emma was asleep on the back porch when Child Protective Services came to take her and her sister from the home. She was young, but not so young that she doesn't think about it every single day. From week to week, she dreads the call or text from a relative informing her of the latest tragedy in her mother's life.

Adalyn's birth mother didn't want her. She was adopted into what seemed to be a loving home, but, that relationship didn't work out. The new stepmom made her want to be back in an orphanage. The physical and sexual abuse would ultimately crush her.

Colton remembers the day, the place, and the exact moment that the oppressive spirit first whispered in his ear. "You're no good. You'll never make it to heaven. If people really knew who you were, they would despise you. You are a pervert, a disgrace." Maybe some would shake off the enemies' attack of condemnation, or have someone to help them. Colton dealt with it alone for years before he cried out for help. He begged God to take his life rather than going on with the struggle.

It shook my world when approximately twenty-four hours after our Sunday service, Julia's father found her dangling from the end of a rope. No note. No warning. No explanation. She survived. We're still in shock.

I grew up in a traditional, two-parent, middle-class home. My brother and I were raised with peace, love, and biblical truth. We had the benefit of a wonderful church and private education. And I'm still weird! I am horrified by the tragedies that so many of our teens have had to endure, but I am amazed by the strength and heart they possess. Because God has been so good to me, I want to give back to Christ by offering leadership to a group of wonderful students who are precious and gifted, but often times broken.

The examples I've shared aren't uncommon. Sit at a theme park and watch them walk past by the hundreds. Around dismissal time, drive slowly past a Jr. High or High School in your community. They are broken, abused, bound, and hurting. Like tortured souls on death row, they slowly proceed towards their end, silently hoping for an unlikely pardon. We have the truth, and it will set them free.

4 - Defining a Youth Counterculture

The term, counterculture, was popularized in Theodore Roszak's 1969 book, *The Making of a Counterculture*. Roszak deals primarily with the American youth culture of the sixties. I'm borrowing the word, not the philosophy. Dictionary.com defines the term as: "the culture and lifestyle of those people, especially among the young, who reject or oppose the dominant values and behavior of society." The young etymologists over there in Oakland, CA have it half right. Here's my definition: a group of people who have chosen to pursue God without regard to where that places them in society.

There are two key elements here: the pursuit of one thing and the alienation from another. A countercultural youth ministry must, by its nature, be estranged from much of what the world would consider normal for teens: premarital sex, homosexuality, materialism, self-centeredness, apathy, disrespect, pride, humanism, sports-fanaticism, and the vast majority of secular music, movies, television, and the Internet. It's necessary to let these things go because a man, or a teen, cannot serve two masters (Luke 16:13). You can't indulge carnal passions and pursue God simultaneously. I'm not moralizing here. Abandoning the world is part of an equation that can be witnessed in the simplicity of a monkey trap. A monkey trap is a pot with a tapered rim, chained to a stake. A monkey reaches into the pot for whatever bait is inside. After grasping the contents inside, the monkey cannot get its hand back out of the pot. The monkey has to let go of the bait in order to escape. Carnality traps teens in a lifestyle of meaninglessness, guilt, and misery. They have to release the bait.

The ultimate aim is the pursuit of God. A countercultural youth group will pray, fast, study the Bible, tithe, worship, love their neighbor, give sacrificially, share truth, and trust God in every circumstance. I'm not suggesting a group of perfect robo-Christians. That's why we call it "pursuing" God and not "catching" God.

There are dozens of sub/countercultures that reveal the great lengths to which teens will go to identify with a particular group (i.e. Goths, Metallers, Jocks, Emos). They make great sacrifices—even self-destructive choices—in order to embrace a culture. Many of the examples are absolutely absurd and evil. More often than not, they are satanic, but I also see in the extreme behavior great energy and will that could be used for good. Such energy, passion, and individuality God intends for good.

Gang culture is one that clearly models the principle I'm trying to share:

- **Unique clothing:** Unity of colors, similarity of style - irrespective of trending fashion.
- **Code of honor:** They live by a unique code that governs their decisions and actions.
- **Familial:** Eat together, play together, work together.
- **Mentality of growth:** They want to grow. If you're on their block they want you in the group. If you're not in the group, they don't want you on their block.
- **Loyalty:** Total commitment.
- **Bravery:** Risking your life or your pride is a prerequisite.
- **Tenure:** Once you're in a gang you may have to die to get out.
- **Higher Law:** A willingness to break the law to be in the group.
- **Sacrifice:** Willing to give up personal preferences.
- **Language:** Members talk the talk.
- **Common lifestyle:** Dropping out of school, drugs, and violence.
- **Leadership:** Members submit, leaders take charge.

- **Ascension:** Everyone wants to grow in respect and responsibility.
- **Discipline:** When the gang rides, so do you.
- **Philosophical consistency:** The gang is what it is. If you want to be a part, you change.

Lets now take a look at the same list with a countercultural youth group perspective.

The Countercultural Youth Group Culture
- **Unique clothing:** Willing to dress modestly according to a godly standard.
- **Code of honor:** Doing what's right by biblical standards, rather than taking their cues from a degenerate culture.
- **Familial:** Eat together, play together, work together, worship together, and pray together.
- **Mentality of growth:** They want to grow. If you're on their block they want you in the church. They are focused on reaching the world because they believe that God's Kingdom is the best thing around.
- **Loyalty:** Total commitment to God and to the church.
- **Bravery:** "He that loseth his life for my sake shall find it" (Matthew 10:39).
- **Tenure:** Once you're in, you're in, and we don't want you to leave.
- **Higher Law:** A higher law than self-will or self-preservation. Submitting to God's Word in everything.
- **Sacrifice:** Willing to give up personal preferences.
- **Language:** Controlling the tongue. Sharing the truth. Glorifying God.
- **Common lifestyle:** Attending church, attending youth events, going to church camp every year.
- **Leadership:** Members submit, leaders take charge.
- **Ascension:** Members want to be faithful in a few things so that God can trust them to be rulers over many (Matt 25:23).
- **Discipline:** "Casting down imaginations, and every high thing that exalteth itself against the knowledge of God, and

bringing into captivity every *thought* to the obedience of Christ" (2 Corinthians 10:5).

- **Philosophical consistency:** The church belongs to God. He establishes what it is. If you want to be in the Kingdom, you have to do it His way.

These are some basic examples. You can find many other applicable traits in various other countercultures.

There's another way to approach youth ministry. The youth pastor studies various elements of pop-culture and tries to include them in his speech, dress, and lifestyle. Phrases like "drop it like it's hot" are intermingled with trendy religious phrases like "let's give God vertical praise." This is intended to show the group that he/she is relevant.

Services and events are organized to appeal to the various sub-groups. Youth events are scheduled around high school sports programs. Music and motif appeal to various and opposite members of the group. Popular music, movies, and television programming are used extensively in activities and sermons/talks.

Teens are encouraged to be who they are, value themselves, and accept failure as a natural course. Services are short and non-confrontational to avoid offending or tiring people. Little is expected. After all, these are just teens. They will most certainly be sowing wild-oats. They can't do much praying, fasting, Bible reading, or soul-winning.

Imagine the gang manufactured around these standards. We'll call our gang the Eclectics. I know, it's not very gang-ish, but it's the best I could do. Our leader will take a survey of all potential gang member to find out what kind of gang they would like to have. All suggestions will be included in the final standards. The leader will work to appeal in a variety of ways to each member of the gang. The colors will be … well, whatever color each member would like to wear. And no one is allowed to judge any other member over things like unity, loyalty, or cohesion. Gang-related events will be held at convenient times for all members. Attendance is optional. Sports programs, church services, birthday parties, and most other event schedules will be respected. All gang events will be canceled in case of inclement weather. K-Love, Corn Country, and the "Kenny G" station can all be blasted from 20 inch subwoofers while cruising the neighborhood. Each member of the group is encouraged to act in whatever way appeals to them. Steal cars and spray paint trains, or brush up on your ballet skills. Every lifestyle is accepted in this gang.

I know I'm being absurd, but the analogy is at least partially applicable. That gang would be the laughing stock. No one would join. It would not do what gangs do. It would not survive. If it did survive, what was left could not be called a "gang." You might call it a social club or a variety group, but not a "gang." Neither will a youth group, built on a similar set of principles, survive. If it does manage to survive, it will not be recognizable as part of God's Kingdom.

I don't want to build a loose-knit group of quasi-Christians. I can't spend precious years herding carnal brutes, disguised as sheep, off a cliff into universities where 80% will be slaughtered by secular humanism before they can add a B.A. to their names.

Not every circumstance will end in victory. Not every student will rise to the mark of the high calling. Reality is an unremitting teacher. I also know that a countercultural youth group is not idealism. It is the will of Christ. God is seeking seekers. God is searching for teens that will worship in spirit and in truth. He's looking for a twelve year old prayer warrior, a fifteen year old soul winner, a seventeen year old that will stand against the tide, and a youth group that will fight together, worship together, love each other, and love Him. He's seeking a group that the world can see coming from a mile away, who will turn that world upside-down. I believe that I am presiding over a group, currently disguised as average teens, who are the next generation of missionaries, church-planters, and pillars of the faith. Give them ten years and they'll prove it. They are a Countercultural Youth Group.

5 - A Divergent Perspective

Here I want to address a dissenting opinion. One might ask: Shouldn't leaders immerse themselves in the culture of those being led in order to better connect with them? Shouldn't they mirror what the teens watch, listen to, how they dress, their language, et cetera? Shouldn't the group identify and feel comfortable with the leader? Shouldn't the leader create a program that appeals to the nature of the largest possible group? Wouldn't that make more teens want to be at church or youth events? Isn't that what any good political head would do?

A great politician needs to be a realist, a pluralist, and an arbiter. First, he needs to be a realist. He has to strive for what *can* be done, rather than for the idealistic. The idealist wants a new bridge that will make a statement to every citizen that sees it. The realist works to get the old bridge painted. What is realistic to expect from teenagers?

Second, he needs to be a pluralist. Merriam-Webster describes pluralism as, "a situation in which people of different social classes, religions, races, etc., are together in a society but continue to have their different traditions and interests." What could we do to establish a program that embraces everybody and every ideology?

Third, he needs to be an arbiter. On every issue there are those who hold one view and others who hold an opposite view. An arbiter finds a synthesis of the two views in an attempt to make the largest number of people happy. How can a youth minister build a team where everybody can hold different views and everybody also be right?

You may be thinking that the above paragraph completely contradicts everything I've said up to this point. It does, and for good reason! We are *not* politicians! We are the called of God. We are tasked with preaching the gospel. Let me quote Jesus, who quoted Isaiah in Luke 4:18-19. "The Spirit of the Lord is upon me, because he hath anointed me to preach the gospel to the poor; he hath sent me to heal the brokenhearted, to preach deliverance to the captives, and recovering of sight to the blind, to set at liberty them that are bruised, to preach the acceptable year of the Lord."

We don't have the option to manufacture a gospel that works for us or the people we lead. We can't make arbitrary decisions about how the lives of the people we lead should look. Those decisions have already been made and recorded in the Bible.

The gospel writer Matthew expresses, "And it came to pass, when Jesus had ended these sayings, the people were astonished at his doctrine: For he taught them as one having authority, and not as the scribes" (Matthew 7:28-29). Jesus' words are the final authority. We have to figure out what He said and mirror it. It's interesting that this passage specifically says He did not speak like the scribes who were, in essence, politicians. Matthew Henry's commentary expounds on this verse: "… they [the scribes] spake as those what were not themselves masters of what they preached: the word did not come from them with any life or force; they delivered it as a school-boy says his lesson; but Christ delivered his discourse, as a judge gives his charge."[3]

We are not called to be video, web, and T-shirt design experts with a minor in Christian website lessonology. The Word and power of God can't be afterthoughts added once our marketing strategy has been established.

Jesus was no politician. He was the ultimate authority. He crashed into the politically religious world of the Jews with astounding words; "let the dead bury their dead," "go and sell all that you have," "go and sin no more," "put up again thy sword," "love not the world." Then He said; "take up your cross," "love God with all your heart," "love your neighbor as your self."

He wasn't a realist, a pluralist, or an arbiter. He didn't use politics to reach the world. He used the power of the Spirit: healing, miracles, and the word of knowledge and revelation to disclose something that almost no one wanted to believe—the truth. But, before all was said and done, He started a fire that burns to this day and brighter than ever.

He is the final Judge, and He has given His charge. We are the ministers of His Word. It may seem counterintuitive. It may seem a couple thousand years out of fashion. But, if it was good enough for Jesus ….

Our purpose is to be like Him, to do what He did.

---

[3]Matthew Henry, J.B Williams, Exposition of the Old and New Testament, Volume 3 (Lausanne, Switzerland: University of Lausaanne, 1838), 57.

Section One
Becoming a Countercultural Leader

6 - Becoming

The most important thing we have is the message of the Bible. Second only to that is the messenger. Before there can be a countercultural youth group, there has to be a countercultural leader. The truth is, youth ministry is not nearly as much about what methods you employ to present the gospel as it is about who you are. Regardless of presentation, who you are will eventually preach your loudest sermon. When that revelation comes, it will galvanize or undermine the message that you've preached.

If you want a countercultural youth group, you have to be radically different than just about anybody else on the planet. You can't be a mundane minister, pretending to be passionate on Sunday. You have to be a revolutionary spirit trying to pretend to be normal enough not to freak people out from Monday to Saturday.

Think about the people in world and church history that really made a difference. Think about the people that you respect the most. When you look at that list, would you describe them in terms like: "normal" in their day, made people feel comfortable, amassed large followings by not offending anybody? If one of the people on your list walked into the room right now, would you say, "I like them because they are just like me?"

What is it that we respect about men like George Washington, Abraham Lincoln, Martin Luther, Hudson Taylor, or John Edwards? What is it about Paul that makes his life so compelling? If you made a list of his attributes, what would they be? Can those attributes be ascribed to you? Of course we aren't Paul. But, he "... was a man subject to like passions as we are..." (James 5:17)

I'm not suggesting that our greatness will change the world. I'm saying that *God's* greatness ought to change *us*. That change in us will do two things: it will prove beyond question the veracity of what we preach, and it will allow the power of God to work through us. (James 5:13-17)

Because you are reading this book, I assume that you are involved with ministry, and that you are practicing spiritual disciplines. However, the indispensable nature of our personal relationship with and commitment to Christ demands that I expound upon them. I will take two chapters dealing with the subject of "becoming." First, we will talk about prayer. I intend to show you that an hour of prayer every day is "our reasonable service." If you only read one more chapter in this book, please read chapter seven. It is the pivotal element of youth ministry. I will explain why in that chapter.

A final word before we embark upon "becoming." I think most of us want to be great. Our motives, for the most part, are pure. Our heroes—Moses, David, Paul—are all perceived as great. We want to be like them. We want to stand at the edge of the water and triumphantly raise our staff and see the waters part. We'd like to ride triumphantly through town with the giant's sword, and maybe even his head. However, becoming a countercultural leader is not about being great. In fact, your becoming great is a contradiction to everything Christ is trying to do. He is great and He will not share His glory with anyone. Don't strive for greatness. Strive to do things that allow God to be great in your world. For starters, pray.

7 - Becoming Through Prayer

"And he went a little further, and fell on his face, and prayed…" (Matthew 26:39).

Jesus went farther than his disciples, physically and spiritually. He went to a place they could not go. If we will take the time and make the effort to go before God in prayer, He will go to places where He is needed the most. He will go beyond closed doors and barred windows. He will enter into the broken places of the heart. He has never hesitated to traverse dark streets and shabby houses. He will slip into the cold and dark places of despair, abuse, and addiction. He will heal, deliver, and save. If you will go where *you* can in prayer, He will go where you *can't*.

Why Pray - My Personal Revelation

I grew up in a wonderful mid-western, Pentecostal family. Memories of kneeling beside my father in our church prayer room will always be with me. I can still hear the resonance of his voice and the phrases often used as he called upon God. My mother's intercessory prayer is the stuff of legend and humor. She prays like no one I've ever known, with deep cries that rock the soul. She often prays for people she does not know. And where she prays she does not care. She prays in the living room, which caused my brother and me to come running more than once. It sounded like the end of the world. We were relieved to discover that mom wasn't dying; she was just praying. That was much better than when she was under a spirit of intercession in a restaurant, or when we had friends over. The fondest memories of my mother aren't vacations, or the food she cooked, although she did make a mean hamburger-helper. The lasting impression is her praying. Because I know my mother will not always be here, a question weighs on my soul: Who will pray her prayers?

You'd think, growing up in that environment, I would have been a man of prayer. Add to that four years of Bible College. The reality could be summed up in the first few words of a poem I wrote as a freshman in high school:

> Another day I failed to pray
> I found other things to do
> Another day I fell by the way
> The troubles I couldn't go through

I graduated from college, got married, started a family, and entered ministry without learning how to pray. I knew the rituals, but I wasn't touching heaven, just appeasing my conscience. For many years I lead a group of thirty to fifty teenagers. I organized events, coordinated services, and preached. I even entered youth leadership over a part of Indiana for several years. All the while I never learned to pray. I held a position in our church and a license with a religious organization, but never learned to pray.

My screen blurs from tears this very moment, as I recall the names of precious young people that are lost today. I know that everyone has free will, and they have all made their choices, but, I also know that I failed. I failed them. I failed God. I was blind, leading the blind, and they did perish. If there was one thing I would go back and do differently, I wouldn't have better events, trendier music, more clever lessons, more cutting-edge graphics or videos, or better youth trips. The one thing I would do is pray. I would pray that God would deliver me from besetting sins. I would lose my will in His purpose. I would lay aside the weights of pride, jealousy, and ambition. I would humble myself before the God that saves.

I would call out the names of the kids. I would soak the floor with my weeping and bombard heaven with my hope. I would stop doing whatever it was that sapped my time and passion. I would pause every other thing in life, and I would pray.

- Moses prayed, and God's wrath abated.
- Joshua prayed, and the sun stood still.
- Hannah prayed, and God gave her a son.
- David prayed, and God forgave him.
- Solomon prayed, and God's presence filled the temple.
- Elijah prayed, and fire fell.
- Daniel prayed, and God closed the lions' mouths.
- Jesus prayed, and disciples were kept from evil.
- Paul and Silas prayed, and the prison was opened.

I have total confidence that the dreams and visions in the Bible were from God, but I get pretty skeptical when people today claim to have a similar experience. On that note, I want to share a dream that I believe was from God. In the dream God spoke to me and said, "You will never have the things you want until I get from you the things that I want." He said that He dangled success in front of my face like a carrot. He motivated me with my hope, but He could never let me attain what I hoped *for*. He said that I worked hard, but that He didn't know why. He wasn't sure if I would continue to work if I got the things I wanted. The dream rocked my world. I knew immediately that God was calling me to a commitment of prayer.

I began to ask God how much prayer he would ask of me. I remembered as a teenager hearing a great missionary, Harry Scism, say, "I don't know how anyone can call themselves a Christian unless they pray an hour a day." God brought that challenge back to me, and I knew I had my answer.

Consider the idea of tithing your margin time (time not spent sleeping, working, going to school, et cetera) in prayer. For a seven-day week, that equals about an hour a day. I'm not suggesting that Scripture commands an hour of prayer a day. I think you can be a Christian and pray less. However, I am absolutely sure that an hour a day is what God was asking from me. If you'll give me the rest of this chapter, I will present my argument for one in twenty-four (an hour of prayer a day). It is possible. It is life changing.

The rule for me is: One hour a day, every day. No excuses. No exceptions. I can't skip today and pray two hours tomorrow. I can't pray two hours today and skip tomorrow. It's similar to manna, except that Sundays aren't excluded from the rule.

Prayer will accomplish many things. I'd like to mention three.

1 - Prayer Will Change You

Over the first few weeks I developed a substantial prayer list. I prayed, among other things, for my wife and my finances to improve. A few weeks passed and I didn't notice much change. Weeks became months before I realized that the first thing God was changing in my life was *me*. God is fundamentally changing who I am. I'm no super Christian. I'm still, "…waiting for the adoption, to wit, the redemption of our body…" (Romans 8:23) But, who I am today is so different as to be unrecognizable to the man I used to be. If you told me today that I would have to continue in ministry without prayer, I would quit. I would not subject myself to the difficulty, or my youth group to the struggle of a ministry without prayer. If there is one thing I would suggest to a young minister it would be this: pray.

2 - Prayer Will Open The Door For Miracles

I have a large cork board in my church office. Early in my new life of prayer, I cut up dozens of pieces of paper, wrote prayer requests on them, and pinned them to the board. One day as I worked my way through the slips of paper, as I often did, I realized that God had answered a prayer. With tears streaming down my face, I moved the request to a new section of the board: "prayers answered." Our Christian school was in its twenty-ninth year without state accreditation. We felt that it was extremely important in order for us to move forward. I was able to move that prayer to the "prayers answered" section.

Our Christian School has lost money for all but one of its thirty-one years. This has been a financial strain on our church. I just looked at our financial report for last year. We had a forty-five thousand dollar turnaround from the last school year, and we were in the black for only the second time in our history. I have now moved that request to prayers answered. It was answered beyond what I asked. Our facility was far too small, and students were having classes in a basement. We needed a new building. Prayer answered. There were needs for healing and needs for restoration. Answered. So many prayers have been answered that I am running out of space on my four by eight foot board. It's hard for me to look at my wall of answered prayers without being overwhelmed by God's goodness. God still does miracles. I'm not suggesting that my prayers are particularly powerful. God is all-powerful, and our prayers express a faith that allows His power to work in our lives.

3 - Prayer Will Save The Lost

My mother claimed a section of our community in prayer. She began walking around several blocks and praying for the people in the houses, businesses, and a church. At the time she was a frail woman after a stroke that could have taken her life but didn't (prayer answered). At times she could barely find the strength to walk, and her prayers felt feeble to her. Within two years of claiming that part of the community, God has allowed her to minister specifically to over a dozen souls. Many have come to church. Two young and underprivileged children have adopted her as their grandmother. She attended cancer treatments with a lonely widow from her prayer walk. People have prayed through to the Spirit. A pastor of a small struggling congregation who's church is within my mother's prayer walk attended one of our church services. With tears in his eyes he approached my father and expressed his deep hurt and need for prayer. A sheriff has been baptized. A backslidden couple is now attending our church faithfully. A new Spanish family is now coming to church. Some of the houses, where drugs abounded, are now empty and awaiting souls receptive to the gospel. All of this from one lady walking around one small, poor area of our community.

Further, while she started praying for those that no one was praying for, her own out-of-state family came back to the Lord.

Are these few blocks special? Did God send my mother to a section of the city that was particularly ripe for revival? Or, is this just one of many areas that have five, ten, twenty, or more people that are desperately in need of an intercessor? Is it possible that block after block in our communities are filled with people that God is waiting for someone to reach in prayer?

In prayer, I have claimed three specific families. As of the writing of this book, I am in a Bible study with one of those families. One family has been baptized and considers themselves to be a part of our congregation. I have not yet invited the third family to church. I am convinced that all eleven of these people are going to be saved. I am also convinced that God has multiplied millions of souls that are ready for salvation. He just needs someone who will pray. "If my people, which are called by my name, shall humble themselves, and pray, and seek my face, and turn from their wicked ways; then will I hear from heaven, and will forgive their sin, and will heal their land" (I Chronicles 7:14).

Can a football coach, with no passion for the game, lead a team to victory? Can a leader, with no passion for revolution, stir a people's hearts for freedom? Prayer is the essence of Christianity. To be the leader of a godly youth counterculture you have to be a person of prayer.

Even if you could inspire a group of teens without prayer, should you? Wouldn't you agree that they need to have a prayer life in order to navigate through life? Paul admonished the Thessalonians, "Pray without ceasing." If you consistently pray, God will revolutionize your life. If you pray, they will pray. If they pray God will revolutionize their lives. Now we are beginning to see a countercultural youth ministry. We're only in the seventh chapter, but we are halfway to our goal.

Finding Time To Pray

The most common argument about prayer is that people don't have the time. Before I tell you why and how you definitely have time to pray, let me make an important clarification. I am a

Pentecostal. I believe in passionate prayer. "...The effectual fervent prayer of a righteous man availeth much" (James 5:16). I believe in speaking in tongues. I believe that prayer is often loud, tearful, and joyful. However, prayer isn't always any of those things, and that is not a bad thing.

Consider this scenario. A man goes to work every day while his wife stays home. After work he returns to the house. As soon as his wife hears the door open she comes running. She leaps into his arms, kisses him profusely, and won't let go. Through tears she expresses how deeply she missed him throughout the day. She promises that she loves him. She repeats her phrases over and over in impassioned tones. This is Monday. Tuesday is the same. Wednesday is the same. Thursday there's no change, and on and on. How would you describe that relationship? Awkward? Forced? Freaky? Nobody is that passionate with that consistency. Perhaps her passion is contrived out of a sense of duty. Maybe it's what she thinks he expects. Maybe she is insecure about the relationship. Perhaps there was an offense committed. The only time most people behave like that is if they have been separated for some time.

Why do we expect ourselves to interact with God in a way that is not natural for humans to behave? Perhaps we think He expects it. Maybe it's been too long since we prayed. Maybe we feel guilty. There is the sports analogy: you yell and scream at a ballgame and then you talk to Jesus like you don't really care. Well, I might go to a ballgame and yell and scream, because that's what everybody else does. I don't scream at libraries, and I don't lack in passion for reading. It's just different. Furthermore, I won't go to a ballgame for an hour a day for the rest of my life.

I'm not suggesting that we talk to God like He's "one of the boys." We owe God deep felt earnestness and respect, but that can be given without contrived emotion. Neither am I suggesting that we never express great passion toward God. The marriage analogy continues to apply. It's perfectly fine with me if upon my arriving home from work, my wife addresses me from over her shoulder while working at the stove. It's okay with me if we have a normal "How was your day?" conversation. However, if that is the only level of passion she ever expresses, we will begin to have a problem. Passion in intimacy is important. It's valuable and meaningful, and it's okay if it happens naturally. I don't expect mechanical or contrived passion. In fact, I don't want it. I approach God in a way that is normal for me. I talk to Him, albeit with great sincerity, as I would a dear friend… who also happens to be God. Quite often, and usually when I least expect it, passion grips my heart and carries me away into the Spirit. Then come the tears and passion. Prayer, even when my mouth is barely moving, is the most heart-rending thing I do. And, I can do it almost any time or anywhere.

After reading the Bible in the morning—We'll talk more about Bible study in a later chapter—I turn on my cellphone stopwatch. I pray as I get ready in the morning. I pray in the car. I pray in the fast-food line to get my oatmeal and water. Throughout the day I can pray while carrying out menial tasks. I love to exercise and pray. I can pray on my bike, on a walk, or on a treadmill in a gym. I can even pray with my family in the car, and usually they don't even know I'm doing it. I love to lay, kneel, or sit and pray. It is a special privilege to find some lonely place and pour my heart out to God. There's really just a handful of things I can't do while praying. Eating and watching entertainment are the most difficult.

When my timer reaches one hour I turn it off. I'm not trying to set prayer records. I'm just trying to make sure I fulfill my commitment. Any time I spend in prayer above an hour is uncharted. Usually I can't get all my prayers prayed in an hour. Prayer is simply amazing. God is amazing. Don't allow unrealistic expectations to keep you from praying. Put aside all pressure concerning prayer except for this one thing: do it.

Still don't feel like you have time to pray? I would challenge you to take a careful inventory of your life. Consider these questions:

Do you have any private time in the morning while you prepare for the day?

Do you have a regular commute?

Do you exercise?

Do you have some margin time in your day that could be redirected?

Hobbies

Overtime

Entertainment

Tasks that could be delegated

If you only have time to do one thing in your day, pray.

What To Pray

The second most common statement I hear in regard to prayer is, "I don't know what to pray for." I often encounter people that don't think they can fill up an hour. Not only do you have enough, you have so much to pray for that you could pray several hours a day and never get it all done. Below is a sample timeline and outline for prayer.

Fifteen minutes
Thanksgiving

I once read a church sign that said, "What if you had tomorrow only the things you thanked God for today?" Sunday schoolish as that may sound, it was revolutionary to me. I attempt to give God heartfelt thanks every day for the things that mean the most to me:

- Family - Mother, father, wife, children, siblings
- List each one and express genuine thoughts of thanks for each.
- Health
- Financial blessings: you can be specific
- Freedom

You get the idea. I could easily spend thirty or more minutes every day in this kind of thanksgiving. In addition, I like to use thanks-series.

- Seven blue things I'm thankful for
- Ten things I'm thankful I don't have
- Five things I'm thankful God has forgiven me for
- Thanks for seasons

Let me give you one abbreviated version of a thanks-series:

3 Physical things I'm thankful for

1 – Light: I exhaust my thoughts on the blessing of physical light. Then I begin to try to thank God for a spiritual equivalent of light. This inevitably is very moving for me.

2 – Water: Expound on the blessings of water

3 – Soil: From the soil comes life, plants, trees, flowers, et cetera. I'm thankful that God has taken the time to work with the soil of my heart... Parable of the treasure... I'm thankful for the seeds of truth that have been planted in my life.

These prayer series are never-ending. There are thousands of possibilities. For me they are very meaningful, enjoyable, and inspirational. They are also very time consuming. I could easily spend an hour on just one series, and the time flies.

Fifteen minutes
Praise and Worship

Thanksgiving tends to honor God for what He does. Praise and Worship honors God for who He is.

- Quoting Scriptures
- Singing songs
- Exalting God's greatness
- Declaring God's goodness
- Dancing
- Silent reverence in awe of His creation, power, mercy
- Exercise faith - Praise for miracles before you see them

Again, this is something you could spend the day doing. You will find that you have to limit yourself in order to get to the other important parts of prayer.

Ten minutes
Repentance

- Confession of your individual, known acts of sin (a lie, an unkind word)
- Confession for your general, ongoing struggles (pride, lust, anger)

- Confession of church or national sins
- Seeking mercy and forgiveness for all of the above
- Ask God to forgive anyone who has wronged you, and pray for God's blessings on them. It's amazing how you care about an enemy when you see them after you have prayed for them. Rather than guilt and anger, there is often a feeling of pity, even love.
- Seek mercy for your family, *youth group,* church, community, state, and nation. Ask for mercy for missionaries and the world. Here is the premise for this prayer; I don't deserve any mercy from God, yet I ask for it and believe I have it. Therefore, I ask God to be merciful to everyone else that doesn't deserve it. "Lord, If you give me mercy, then please give it to them."

Twenty minutes
Prayer for Needs

For the groups below, call out their names, plead the blood of Jesus, pray for God's blessings, deliverance, and help.

Pray for People
- Family - Take a moment and write, from memory, the names of family members. Are they all saved? How many of those unsaved family members have someone praying for them every day? Don't worry about your family; pray for them.
- Your Youth Group
- Youth leadership
- Key young people
- Kids in desperate circumstances
- The lost youth of your community
- Your pastor
- Other ministers in the church
- The church members
- The community
- Neighboring pastors and churches
- Enemies
- Government
- Missionaries

- The unknown and unseen masses around the world

Pronounce God's promises
- Healing
- Truth
- Deliverance
- Joy

Rebuke the devourer in Jesus' name. Bind and rebuke:
- Disease
- False doctrine
- Addictions
- Perversion
- Apathy
- Spiritual blindness

Take the time to express your requests to God. "Ask, and it shall be given you; seek, and ye shall find; knock, and it shall be opened unto you: For every one that asketh receiveth; and he that seeketh findeth; and to him that knocketh it shall be opened" (Matthew 7:7-8). Your daily requests are not selfish redundancy taking up time to fulfill your prayer-quota. Your importunate prayers are an act of faith that will touch the heart of God on behalf of your world. "And I sought for a man among them, that should make up the hedge, and stand in the gap before me for the land, that I should not destroy it…" (Ezekiel 22: 30).

As you exercise faith by asking God for the miraculous, praise is the natural next step. A great way to finish an hour of prayer is praise and worship. By faith we can even praise God as though we have already received the answer to our prayers.

8 - Becoming Through Christian Disciplines

Read The Word

"Then the twelve called the multitude of the disciples unto them, and said, It is not reason that we should leave the word of God, and serve tables. Wherefore, brethren, look ye out among you seven men of honest report, full of the Holy Ghost and wisdom, whom we may appoint over this business. But we will give ourselves continually to prayer, and to the ministry of the word" (Acts 6:2 - 4).

Study The Word Of God

It's more important than marketing, service structure, organization, events, counseling, or communication. It's more important than ministerial relevance or personal style.

God's Word will give you power, keep you from error, make you wise, and make you holy. God's Word will save your youth group, give them strength, nourish their lives, pierce their souls, and give them a song. It's more important than checking your email, reading *this* book, studying that article, or perusing a website. If you can only do two things, pray and read the Word.

I highly recommend the book, "Taking God at His Word," by Kevin DeYoung. DeYoung masterfully portrays the passion that David had for Scripture. If the warrior king, David, cherished God's law so much that he wrote the unmatched poetry of Psalms 119 about the Bible, we ought to consider anew its extraordinary value in our lives. Read it every day. "Give us this day our daily bread..." (Matthew 6:11). God held the Children of Israel in II Kings 22 accountable for the law that was lost, forgotten in the rubble of the temple. How much more does He expect us to have His Word in our hearts? We have Bibles everywhere. We have Google—a powerful tool for searching the Scripture. We have websites like BibleGateway.com and BibleHub.com. We have dozens of apps like BlueLetterBible and YouVersion that are free for the taking. Put them to use. Start a Bible reading plan. Read through the Bible this year. If you study God's Word it will revolutionize your life. If you study God's Word, your youth group will too. If they will, God will revolutionize their lives.

Fasting

If there's anything in the world more countercultural and counter-carnal than prayer, it is fasting. And, there are few things more biblical. I haven't yet met the man who enjoys giving up a meal, a hobby, or some form of pleasure for *any* reason. And yet the rewards are too compelling to overlook. The flesh has to be crucified. "Celebration of Discipline," by Richard J. Foster, will convict and challenge you to make fasting a consistent part of your life.

It's easier to fast with a fasting-buddy. Church or youth group fasts are biblical, unifying, and inspiring.

Fast a meal, fast for a day, fast a particular kind of food, drink, or activity. I prefer to fast on a rotating schedule. Rotating Fast Schedule example:
- Week 1 - fast bread
- Week 2 - fast red meat
- Week 3 - fast entertainment
- Week 4 - fast soda

We fast because it's the right thing to do, and it invokes the hand of God in our lives and ministry. I believe that God's work is done in our students' because of our small sacrifice. We also fast as an example, not to receive glory, but to show its importance. If you fast, God will move. If you fast, they will fast... I think you have the idea.

Separated Lifestyle

"But the day of the Lord will come as a thief in the night; in the which the heavens shall pass away with a great noise, and the elements shall melt with fervent heat, the earth also and the works that are therein shall be burned up.

"Seeing then that all these things shall be dissolved, what manner of persons ought ye to be in all holy conversation and godliness, Looking for and hasting unto the coming of the day of God, wherein the heavens being on fire shall be dissolved, and the elements shall melt with fervent heat?" (2 Peter 3:10 - 12).

I was at a church youth camp in Arkansas in 1993. I was eighteen years old and traveling the country with a Bible School music group. We were trying to be spiritual, but we were young. After we finished singing, the preacher took the floor. He started strong, but then things began to go terribly wrong. In trying to illustrate to the crowd just how crazy the world is, he embarked upon a monologue showing all the ways that people use the word, hell. "It's cold as he**," he mocked. "It's hot as he**. I'm tired as he**. I'm mad as he**. What in the he**? Why in the he**." He went on and on for several minutes, cussing. At some point the members of our little group started looking at each other. The liberated grins revealed that this night was about to get as wild as... well, you know. And it did! I'll never forget the strait-laced and proper young woman, who is now a minister's wife, cussing a blue streak! We absolutely lost our minds and our moral compass for about twenty-four hours before the conviction of the Holy Ghost was able to reign us back in. I said all that to illustrate something we all know; what you do in moderation, they will do in excess. The question is: What kind of things are you modeling in moderation?

As a youth minister, you are working with people at the most vulnerable time in their lives. Children are more impressionable, but they miss a lot. Young adults are perceptive, but they are also more solidified. Teens are picking up on your lifestyle, and they are susceptible to its influence. You are producing younger, and slightly more extreme versions of yourself. Paul said, "Be ye followers of me, even as I also am of Christ" (1 Corinthians 11:1). The first part of that verse is not in question: they *will* follow you. The second part is what we have to ask ourselves: Are we following Christ?

Is Christ Obvious In Our Charity?

In Mark 12:28-31, Jesus reaffirms the importance of His oneness and tells us the second great commandment: "Love your neighbor as yourself."

If you organize the greatest youth events and take students on missions trips and have not love.... If you build youth rooms and have a band that would make "Third Day" proud, and have not love... If you're athletic, well dressed, articulate, and well read, and have not love, it's all smoke and mirrors, and doesn't have God's essence.

The best opportunity I've had to teach love to our students happened *to* me quite accidentally. While driving a van load of teens home from a youth conference the kids talked me into taking them to get frozen yogurt. On the way, a lady stepped into the road and waved her hands in an attempt to get me to stop. I eased my foot on to the gas a little harder and passed on by. On the way back, the twenty-something year old woman again attempted to flag me down. I stopped begrudgingly. I'd been suckered into cons one too many. Gritting my teeth, I stepped out of the van and walked toward the woman. She had returned to her car, so as I approached the vehicle I realized she had two young children with her. I would eventually learn that she had traveled several hours to meet her ex-husband. He had promised to put gas in her car for the return trip, but had stood her up. She had no gas and no money. I saw several empty packages of chips laying in the backseat of the car. I asked the destitute single mother of two if the children had eaten anything other than junk food. They hadn't, and wouldn't any time soon. My irritation melted into guilt and then to motivation. All the teens pitched in, and we drove to a local department store and purchased a gas can. We delivered the gas and gave her money for more fuel and food.

For us, the story ended with a feeling that we had given a cup of cold water to one of "these little ones." I only wished that I had done it on purpose. I *did* learn a valuable lesson.

Love your neighbor. Love your spouse and children. Love the poor and hurting. Love the kids that smell so bad it turns your stomach. Love the popular ones and the ones who sit alone. Love the girls, the boys, young, and old. Love the ones with social value and the ones who can't behave for five minutes at a time. Love them more than you love your car or your house. Love them more than you love your hobbies, money, a secular vocation, even more than you love yourself. Love them enough to pray for them, to preach to them, to correct them, to be proud of them, and to spend time with them. Love them enough to be patient. Love them enough to pay for their meal. Churchill penned the words: "...if necessary for years, if necessary alone." A countercultural youth leader will love the unlovable as long as it takes, even when no one else will, or can.

Is Christ Obvious In The Things We Indulge?

A Christian friend invited me to his house to watch a video that he highly recommended. It truly was a powerful WWII film, except for something that my friend skipped over. I had no idea what we didn't watch. To my knowledge, the film was clean. I learned otherwise, from the incredulous look of a teenaged boy when I told him I had seen the film. His look said several things. First, he couldn't believe that his youth pastor would watch a movie with a "bad" scene. Yes, it had a pretty bad love scene. I was innocent, but that did not matter. Second, the look said, "this lowers the bar on what is acceptable to watch." I went back and tried to explain to the young man what had happened. I'm not sure it helped.

Hollywood purports to mirror what is common in society. Nothing could be farther from the truth. Most movies and television programs betray a clear agenda that has been conceived and is being promoted by the entertainment industry. Consider the television series scenario:

The pilot episode introduces a character. He/she is smart, pretty/handsome, witty, deeply principled, and misunderstood. Over the duration of a season, or seasons, the audience is coaxed into idolizing and/or identifying with the character. At the same time, the character engages in or holds views about moral issues that are well beyond what is socially acceptable even in a secular society (i.e. euthanasia, abortion, homosexuality, murder, prostitution, population control). The audience may struggle with the morally problematic elements of the program or character, but in time, we are enamored by the character's heroic nature. Their virtue eclipses our apprehensions. The dividing line between right and wrong is not being modeled, it is being moved, one episode at a time.

Hollywood hates most of what you believe. They are against most of what you are for. If you are countercultural, they are counter-Christian: antichrist. To my knowledge there are no actor's guilds lobbying for Christian principles. So, why are Christian people tempted to make allowances for them? Every compromise we make sends a signal. Is it a guiding light or a spirit of confusion?

Is the holiness of God obvious through the things we watch? If the students we lead watch programing that is several degrees worse than what we indulge, will their minds be molded by the holy? Are we promoting biblical values or hedonism? They are watching us. They are listening.

Is it possible to encourage students to live to a higher standard then they have seen from preceding generations? I have often preached the principle of a pendulum. In order to keep a pendulum from going back the wrong direction, it must keep moving forward. In preaching to our students, I've used the example of my own family. Going back several generations, you'll find illiteracy, alcoholism, and poverty. My great-grandfather found God, or was found by God and began preaching the truth. Family lore says that though he was illiterate, he was able, miraculously, to read the Bible. My grandfather continued the forward progression of our family. Through great difficulty, living in the poorest part of the United States, grandpa worked hard, and raised his family of seven. He later planted a new church in Florence, Kentucky. My father continued the legacy. He went to Bible College, has worked in Bible College administration, and in the classroom, for over thirty years. He pastors a large and healthy church which has planted several daughter works. I am "standing on the shoulders" of these giants who took great steps of faith. It is my responsibility to arm myself with the commitments of previous generations and march into spiritual battle to take new territory. If they prayed, I must pray more. If they sacrificed, I must give more. If they were faithful, I must rise to new heights. When does this pendulum stop? I pray that it does not stop with me.

I do not criticize past leaders or the families of our young people; rather, I challenge them to keep moving towards God. This type of leadership has to start with us. We have to break the curse of ever-decaying generations by adopting truly biblical holiness into our every day lifestyle.

Is Christ Obvious In The Way We Talk?

"A merry heart doeth good like a medicine..." (Proverbs 17:22). A great sense of humor is an asset to a youth leader. Learn to enjoy the teens you work with. "All ministry and no fun makes a youth pastor a lame duck." Make the kids glad they came. However, "...every idle word that men shall speak, they shall give account thereof in the day of judgment" (Matthew 12:36). God forbid that our youth groups feel encouraged to indulge inappropriate language, learn innuendos, or dirty jokes from us. You don't have to humiliate a teen for crossing the line, but they should always get the sense from you that there *is* a line.

Is Christ Obvious In Our Moderation?

"Let your moderation be known unto all men. The Lord is at hand" (Philippians 4:5). Do they see our moderation by what car we drive, our possessions, how we spend our money, our use of time, the clothes we wear, our physical appearance, our moods, how we correct people, how we praise people, and how we treat our spouse and children?

While we cannot save ourselves through righteousness, we sure can make a major impact upon our students' decision to live for God.

9 - Nothing But the Truth

We have to have an unwavering commitment to truth. We're doing everything we can to win the hearts and minds of students, but what are we winning them to?

Does doctrine really matter? Is it possible that we're making religion more difficult than it should be, even divisive? Are we making mountains out of semantics?

In addition to being a world-class evangelist, D. L. Moody was a noted ecumenicist. Moody broke down the walls of doctrinal differences that separated church denominations. Many would consider this a triumph. Lyle W. Dorsett praised Moody in his book, "A Passion for Souls: The Life of D. L. Moody."

Dorsett recounts Moody's promotion of the work of the little known evangelist and naturalist, Henry Drummond. Drummond's magnum opus, "The Ascent of Man," sought to find a synthesis between the Genesis account of creation and evolutionary biology. According to Dorsett, "Despite the furor that surrounded Drummond when his theistic evolution writings were published, Moody refused to repudiate him."[4] Drummond's work would eventually make a major contribution to Theistic Evolution (TE) being adopted by many denominations. Today, "TE is the view of creation taught at the majority of protestant seminaries, and it is the position of the Catholic Church," according to Eugene Carrol Scott in, "Evolution

Vs. Creationism: An Introduction." If it is true that the majority of protestant seminaries have abandoned Genesis as a factual account of creation, it may also be true that the Bible as the indispensable and indisputable foundation of Christianity is in jeopardy in those seminaries and the bodies they serve. Many believe that the dehumanizing doctrine of evolution played a great role in the slaughter of millions during the holocaust. Furthermore, according to Michael Behe's, "The Edge of Evolution," Darwinian evolution is in need of a major overhaul, even for die-hard evolution advocates. What a tragedy that millions of Christians gave up so much—Genesis—for so little, Darwinian error. Are the particulars of doctrine semantics or the insoluble hope of salvation? "But though we, or an angel from heaven, preach any other gospel unto you than that which we have preached unto you, let him be accursed" (Galatians 1:8).

Don't let go of doctrine to please an individual. Don't let go of truth to gain a crowd. Don't relinquish the Word for all that the world has to offer. "...All these things will I give thee, if thou wilt fall down and worship me. Then saith Jesus unto him, Get thee hence, Satan: for it is written..." (Matthew 4:9-10).

The massive auditorium filled with seekers is a siren call to the ambitious. While their bands regale cardigan clad crowds for the second and third rounds of their Sunday morning services, we hit another chorus of "Nothing but the Blood" before preaching about Jesus' name baptism to our group of forty-five. Like fasting at a neighborhood barbecue, we may be tempted to fall off the wagon and join the crowd.

What are mega-churches serving, and who? There's a lesson to be learned from some thoughts about the Industrial Revolution versus the Walmart Revolution. The Industrial Revolution, from the mid 1700's to the early 1800's, marked a dramatic change in industrial processes. The production of goods increased exponentially. People who previously could scarcely afford many of the essentials of life, now had access to these necessary items at affordable prices. The undervalued masses now found their employment in great demand. It was a true revolution.

Contrast that with what I call the Walmart Revolution. In the past, small businesses, across the United States, have grown along side the towns they service. Bakeries, clothiers, tire shops, hunting stores, and pharmacies, to name a few, owned by locals, with local employees, have served local people for many years. When a Walmart store moves into an area, with its job opportunities and convenient array of services, mom & pop shops begin to close. I'm not criticizing Walmart stores. I like them. However, there are a couple relevant questions: Are Walmart stores selling new or greatly improved products that were not previously being offered? Are super-stores making new customers? Are Walmart customers people who weren't buying groceries somewhere else? Or, are they facilitating the closure of small stores and consolidating customers?

Are mega-churches preaching a gospel that is more biblical? Are they spreading an improved message that is truly revolutionizing communities? Are they reaching people that weren't already being ministered to by other churches? Or, are they making it hard for small churches to survive and then consolidating the disembodied masses? Is it possible that the growth chart of mega-ministries across the country could be flipped upside down to represent the decline of small churches? Is that why God died? Is that why we've accepted a call into ministry? Are we here to build a sharper program that draws current customers into a new venue, where by its very nature, we cannot offer a pure product? "When Jesus heard it, he saith unto them, They that are whole have no need of the physician, but they that are sick: I came not to call the righteous, but sinners to repentance" (Mark 2:17). I'm not suggesting we can't proselytize those that only have partial truth. Preach truth. The truth will set men free from anything less than the fullness of the gospel. Win the world with truth. If we build a crowd with anything less, [we] "... Labor in vain" (Psalms 127:1).

---

[4]Dorsett, Lyle W. (2003-10-01). A Passion for Souls: The Life of D.L. Moody (Kindle Locations 4130-4131). Moody Publishers. Kindle Edition.

10 - Nothing to Fear

The right thing is always the right thing, always, no matter how scary it may be. Teenagers can be intimidating. Incensed parents can put fear in the heart of the most stalwart countercultural leader. But we have to do what is right. We can't change the message to make anyone happy. We must not compromise to avoid confrontation. We cannot backpedal to alleviate backlash.

You're called by God, anointed by the elders, and empowered by education, but you're still going to have to establish yourself in the pecking order. The old west sheriff has to be willing to kick behinds and take names. The dominant buck can't walk away from a challenge. The head rooster has to peck the face off of his nearest rival or have his face pecked off. It's very hard to minister with no face. The work that we are doing is going to mean heaven or hell for many. You owe it to God, and to the people you're responsible for, to earn and maintain your place as the leader. If you show signs of weakness, they will rob you of your ability to lead.

I'm not suggesting that you should be domineering or mean. To the contrary, in a later chapter we will focus on the necessity for meekness and love. I'm saying that, with love, meekness, and kindness, you hold the line of what is right and don't give one inch.

You *will* be challenged, "Be not afraid of their faces: for I am with thee to deliver thee, saith the LORD" (Jeremiah 1:8).

So, it's established, we're going to stand our ground. What ground are we going to stand on? How do we know what the right thing is?

First, the Bible is always right. We have to make Bible study a part of our everyday lives. Second, we have to pray. Third, we should seek council.

When you're faced with a challenging situation that will affect people in the church, talk to your pastor. Seeking godly wisdom will help you find the line between your anger or pride, and the will of God. Anger and pride are both blinding forces. It's never good to make any decisions while you're flailing blindly. I never want our pastor to be forced to clean up my messes. So, I get him involved in making the mess.

After you establish what is right, proceed with wisdom in the fear of God. Here are some suggestions to live by:

- Don't humiliate people
- Don't use the church as your personal bully pulpit
- Avoid publicly calling people out by name or specific situations
- Don't overstep your bounds. Challenge kids without undermining parents
- Don't speak in anger
- Treat every student the way you'd want someone to treat your own child
- Correct teens as God's children, not like a gardener pulling weeds
- Choose your battles
- Preach the Word consistently

It's easy to get suckered into battles that have no value to the kingdom. Author, Gary Gagliardi writes, "Defeating or surpassing our opponents can be useful, but only if it improves our position.

Beating opponents does us no good if it leaves us in a worse position than before. The goal is only to improve our position over time."[5] Here is a question that should be asked before going into any church conflict: When I win this battle, will the Kingdom of God be in a better place than it is now? If the answer is yes, with your pastor's approval, with the Word, prayer, meekness and love, proceed without fear—God is with you.

------

[5]Gary Gigliardi, Sun Tzu's The Art of War Plus The Warrior Class: 306 Lessons in Strategy, (Seattle Washington: Clearbridge Publishing, April 21, 2014), 19.

11 - The Spirit of Meekness ... Not Weakness

There is no place for insecurity in youth ministry. You have to have confidence in your programs, your ideas, your sermons and lessons, your choices, your advice, and yourself in general. If you don't *have* confidence, act like you do! If you don't at least act like you know what you're doing, they will assume you don't, and one or more of them will assert their authority in your place. Make decisions and go with it.

What decisions should you make and stand by?
- What game to play
- How to choose teams
- What time to start
- What time an event will end
- What songs to sing
- Who will play in the band
- Where to eat... especially where to eat
- What lessons to teach
- How the group will read the Bible
- Who sits where in the van
- And a million other things

If this sounds like tyranny, well, it is. Youth ministry is not a democracy. You have to make the decisions. Why? Because any time you give them an option, like where to eat, the group will be divided. No matter which part of the group wins the decision, the other part will feel slighted and you will be accused of favoritism. Nip this in the bud and make arbitrary decisions about everything without input from any teen. When they have *good* ideas, ignore them. I'm saying this only partly in jest. Really, you have to make all the decisions. Meekness is a virtue. Weakness is a prelude to DISASTER!

If you struggle with insecurity, you are not alone. Maybe you struggle with low self-esteem. Maybe you feel old, bald, fat, ugly, or out of style. Well, you probably are. Join the club. Maybe your parents didn't show you enough affection, maybe your spouse is cold and distant, maybe you are 39 and nowhere near where you thought you'd be at this stage in your life. Pray about it, get some counseling, find an accountability partner. Whatever you do, do *NOT* bring your emotional needs into your ministry. I understand emotional issues… I have them too. Check them at the door.

- Your students are not here to be your "friends."
- Your students are not here to make you feel loved.
- The youth group isn't your support group.
- These teens are not here to make you feel smart or important.
- They are not here to praise your ideas, programs, or sermons.
- Your group isn't here to make you feel like a hero.
- You aren't the Savior: gaining self-worth with every super-human act.
- These students are not here to counsel you about your marriage.
- They aren't your buds to hang out with.

You have to understand your position. You are a called man or woman of God, sent to administer the Word to a group of young people. They need a confident leader to imbue God's Word into their lives. You may feel insecure, but remember Moses' altercation with his sister. You must acknowledge and respect the position that God has put you in.

With all that said, it is critical that you possess and exhibit a spirit of meekness. "Now the man Moses was very meek, above all the men which were upon the face of the earth" (Numbers 12:3). "Blessed are the meek: for they shall inherit the earth" (Matthew 5:5). "The LORD is nigh unto them that are of a broken heart; and saveth such as be of a contrite spirit" (Psalms 34:18). We have to be meek in order to have the favor of God, to earn the respect of our students, and to model Christ-like behavior worth emulating.

Have Meekness Before God

David said, "For I acknowledge my transgressions: and my sin is ever before me" (Psalms 51:3). Paul admonished a man "...not to think of himself more highly than he ought to think" (Romans 12:3). I consider it a vital part of my walk with God, to frequently recount to myself and my creator the reasons why I don't deserve salvation, let alone glory. Any instance of pride in me is not only sin, it is pure delusion. Only in my own personal fantasy world do I deserve anything that God has given me. I am in ministry because of God's mercy and for His purpose.

Have Meekness With Your Pastor

A common feature of youth ministry is frustration with a pastor. You may think your pastor is old, outdated, unprogressive, budget oriented, dream-smashing, program-killing, slow-moving, and a killjoy. You're not the first youth pastor to be frustrated. Our only response to all these flaws is meekness. "Obey them that have the rule over you, and submit yourselves: for they watch for your souls, as they that must give account, that they may do it with joy, and not with grief: for that is unprofitable for you" (Hebrews 13:17).

Let me give you an exhaustive list of reasons that you have to show meekness and submit to your pastor:

1. God won't bless your ministry if you don't.
2. God won't bless your ministry if you don't.
3. God won't bless your ministry if you don't.

We should also at least *consider* the possibility that we aren't always right and they aren't always wrong. In most cases, they have more experience than we do. Our cutting-edge breakthrough may just be a rehash of an idea that they saw miserably fail in 1972.

In many cases, the pastor has won to God the families whose children you now lead. He baptized them. He prayed them through to the Holy Spirit. He dedicated them. He was there when they suffered. He was in the waiting room when the doctor solemnly announced, "they didn't make it." Pardon that old man if he doesn't automatically trust every brilliant idea that you have. He was investing his blood, sweat, and tears in these people when you were picking your noes in preschool.

Be meek enough to patiently earn the trust of the pastor. Gently cast your ideas to him, like a lure. If he's not interested, try something else. Take him to lunch and test the waters with a concept. If he shows an inclination to listen, invite him to the conference room and present your program in detail. Let him think about it. If at first he rejects it, try again… later… much later. If it's really God's will, won't God work on him? If your pastor is impervious to God's voice, maybe you're in the wrong place. Warning, that kind of verdict takes years of deliberation. Excepting obvious moral failure, spiritual aptitude is hard to discern. Be patient.

Consider this scenario:

You want to have youth services during Wednesday Bible Studies. That seems like an obviously good idea to you. Maybe it is. Now, who is going to teach or preach in your youth service? You? Who teaches the Wednesday Bible Study? Him? Let me summarize what you're saying: He's been teaching Wednesday night Bible Study for years, but his teaching is irrelevant and sub-par. The kids aren't getting anything from it. They would be better off with a much younger and better speaker who will make all the difference in their lives, namely, you. You want him to continue to spend his Wednesdays studying, but now he'll only have half the audience, the old half. Sure, I can see how he'll be thrilled about this proposition.

Be meek enough to put yourself in his shoes. The bottom line is that he will be right much, or even most, of the time. When he isn't right, consider the factors that might lead to his error. Maybe he doesn't trust you. But you've been the youth pastor for three weeks, and you have an associates degree from a Bible college. Earn his trust. This takes time.

Be patient. One of the reasons for a dearth of great youth programs is a lack of young men or women willing to "stick it out." It's almost impossible to know what your true potential is in the first three months, or even three years.   If, after giving a pastor ample time to allow you to minister, he proves to be resistant to everything you try to do, you may have to leave. Our options are as follows: Humbly submit with patience and loyalty, or leave. These are the only two scenarios God can bless.

Show Meekness To The Other Leaders In The Church

The pastor that you have determined to respect has probably appointed a staff to aid in the work of ministry. Let the meekness and loyalty you give to the pastor extend to his staff. Jockeying has no place in the church. If you're the man, God will make that apparent. If there is a Judas in the group, Jesus will take care of it. Love, respect, support, promote, and pray for the ministers in the church. You are setting a great example for your students to follow, and God will bless you.

It is good for students to have multiple spiritual influences in their lives. Encourage other ministers in the church to engage with the youth group. The church should not be an ambition driven, they're with Paul and they're with Apollos, situation. We're all working to build the same kingdom.

Respect the schedule. Plan the youth program in December and get all events on the calendar for the following year. Communicate with other ministries within the church. Resolve schedule conflicts with meekness.

Be thoughtful when using shared assets like church vans, classrooms, and the gym. Leave things better than you found them. If you break something, own up to it and make it right. Don't leave church vehicles on "empty" for the next group that needs to use them.

Show Meekness When Dealing With Parents

Don't side with kids against their parents. Don't undermine the authority of parents. Don't overstep your authority. Treat the parents of your students the way that God expects your teenagers to treat their moms, dads, and stepparents. Communicate with families. Work to maintain a healthy relationship with them. Resolve conflicts as much as it is within your power. You may win an argument with a parent and lose the battle for their child's soul. Having parents realize how much smarter you are than they are has little or no value. However, having them allow you to influence their kids is priceless.

Exhibit Meekness Toward Your Students

This is the most complicated aspect of meekness we'll address. Yes, I'm saying be a dictator and be meek. How can you do that? It's not as much something you will *do*, but rather it is what you *are*. You recognize your position. You exercise your authority. You make decisions and stand by them. At the same time you acknowledge to God your unworthiness to carry out the task. You consider the lives of your students more important than your own. You recognize the great value that God places on every young person you encounter. Even "the least of these" are God's dearest children. They are worthy of respect, love, and determined effort. They are worth your time. Be patient with their ignorance, immaturity, and sin. Speak gently to them unless they're about to walk off a cliff. True meekness toward them will be perceived by them. They will love you for it and follow you rather than resist. Meekness is not a normal quality. It is, in fact, countercultural. Meekness is that kind of characteristic that inspires teens.

12 - The Fallacy of Authenticity

The concept of being "authentic" in many ways is great. We have to be in reality what we appear to be. However, there is another side of authenticity that isn't only wrong, it's disastrous. Being a countercultural youth leader does not mean that we should strive to be our "authentic selves." Being authentic, or true to yourself, is a fallacy. What does it really even mean? Does authenticity require grumpy people to be obtuse? Does it mean that a guy who struggles with lust should go ahead and fornicate? Is the girl that struggles with jealousy required to go ahead and cut her "friends" down to size? Maybe the man who struggles with dishonesty should lie as a point of principle. Being "authentic" is a sure method to failure unless your name is Jesus. We absolutely cannot allow our natural impulses, or raw personality, to play out in whatever way seems natural.

As ministers, our lives are almost always on display. Most professions stop making demands on an employee when the clock is punched at the end of the day. However, there are a handful of vocations that offer little or no reprieve. Youth ministry falls into this second category. What we do "on the field" is extremely important. But just as significant is who we are on our day off. Most of us wouldn't take the pulpit on a Sunday with no thought of what we're going to say. Neither should we take the stage of life hoping to improvise our way through.

Of course we have a personal life. We can, in privacy, share our hurt, anger, and doubt with our spouse or a confidential friend. We should all work to cultivate relationships that allow us to be honest or accountable. However, we can't ever punch-out at the end of a youth class or event and become Mr. Hyde. We can't preach our guts out and then "let our hair down" with inappropriate humor or self-centeredness. We have a part to play when we speak as the oracle of God, and a part that we play when we're picking up our laundry. We are on the clock quite nearly all the time. And, for most of that time, we are on parade in some way or another.

Authenticity is a real problem when you consider Jeremiah 17:9: "The heart is deceitful above all things, and desperately wicked: who can know it?" If we're all authentic, the world is in trouble. I'm thankful that there are desperately wicked people who are NOT true to themselves.

Forrest McDonald, research professor of history at the University of Alabama, touched on the subject of authenticity in an address given in 1995. McDonald explained the impact that Joseph Addison's play, Cato, had on George Washington in his formative years. "… its message was clear: Addison advised young Washington to follow precisely the opposite course from that recommended by Shakespeare's Polonius. In Hamlet, Polonius says: 'This above all: to thine own self be true, and it must follow, as the night the day, thou canst not then be false to any man.' Shakespeare put those words in the mouth of a prattling fool, and Addison's message is that, for public man, they are foolish words. Rather, he says: Do not trust in your own righteousness. Instead, be true to others; seek the esteem of the wise and the good, and it follows that you cannot then be false to yourself—or to your country."

McDonald continued: "The term 'character' was rarely used in the eighteenth century as we use it, to refer to internal moral qualities. Rather, at least in polite society and among people in public life, it referred to a persona or mask that one deliberately selected and always wore: one picked a role, like a part in a play, and sought to act in that role unfailingly, ever to be in character. If one chose a character with which one was comfortable, and if one played it long enough and consistently enough, it became a 'second nature' that in practice superseded the first. One became what one pretended to be.

"Washington chose to play a progression of characters, each grander and nobler than the last, and he played them so successfully that he ultimately transformed himself into a man of almost extra-human virtue."

There are two kinds of ministry in which we engage. First, overt ministry is composed of the things we study for and orchestrate. It's the lessons we teach, the curriculum we employ, the programs we promote, the sermons we preach, and the events we plan. Our overt ministry is contrived and calculated.

The second type is covert ministry. This is the part of our lives that is not necessarily done behind a pulpit or while engaging in a specific program. It is our demeanor, the way we dress and communicate, the way we treat our spouse and children, our work ethics, our personal walk with God, financial choices, and much more. Our covert ministry must also be contrived and calculated.

Through God's Word and by studying mentors, we need to determine what it will take to win souls and please God. Once we figure out what that is, we need to abandon our nature and strive for perfection.

It is right and necessary for you to mask your natural inclinations and deliberately create a persona that you'll spend a lifetime trying to perfect. This is not hypocrisy, it is obedience to Scripture. "Casting down imaginations, and every high thing that exalteth itself against the knowledge of God, and bringing into captivity every thought to the obedience of Christ" (2 Corinthians 10:5). If any man among you seem to be religious, and bridleth not his tongue, but deceiveth his own heart, this man's religion is vain" (James 1:26). So much for authenticity. Not only are we to control what we say, we are commanded to control even what we think. Without a constant check, we will default to our carnal nature—a disaster.

You've had a long youth event. You're tired, it's late, and you still have a couple kids to take home. You cannot relax and be yourself. You can pretend to relax, feign being yourself, but keep the show going. Don't share with the other youth your frustration about a kid that was acting out during the event. Don't get mad because you have to drive twenty minutes out of your way at midnight because a girl left her purse at the church. I know that ignorant girl would leave her head if it wasn't attached. Pretend! Pretend you like being out in the middle of the night after a long day instead of warm in your bed. Pretend that you are excited about the service Sunday. Talk about ministry. Pretend you are interested in their love lives, family problems, and petty passions. Express emotions you don't feel. Share faith you don't presently have. Covert ministry is often the "substance of things hoped for and the evidence of things" you don't feel. I know that June Cleaver was an actor. But I'd wager that she influenced millions of young girls to cook, and clean, and dress nice even if their own mothers didn't. Be what they need you to be for their sake even if it's not natural for you. I am not my own. My soul has been purchased at a great price, and I owe my life, every moment of it, to God. I want every part of my life and ministry to express truth and the love of Christ to the people that God has given me.

13 - Love Your Students

The greatest part of loving is accomplished when you crucify your flesh in order to "become" the person your students need. You pray, study the Word, and discipline your flesh, in part, because you love *them*. I want to look at some other ways to express that love as well as ways *not* to.

Love Them With Your Time

Probably the most powerful way you will express your love is by giving your students the most precious thing you possess: time. Be at the youth services, events, and classes. Don't be the last to arrive and pushing for the event to end. Make sure that your absence is the exception, not the rule. If you walk in to a youth event and they are surprised, you have a problem.

Value the time you have with your students. Maybe playing hide-and-seek doesn't seem too crucial to their development. You won't have bragging rights with your college buds because you broke the all-time hiding record by concealing yourself and fifteen teenagers in the ceiling for two hours. Just remember that you are smashed into a dark and dirty, potentially spider-infested space with future missionaries, church-board members, pastors, and intercessors. They are extraordinary, and your godly influence *away* from the pulpit is powerful. But this all takes time.

Plan non-church related activities every week. Eat, play, and laugh with them. Share your heart with them. More importantly, let them share theirs with you. Most of the time, we are doing all the talking. During a youth event you can listen. Let them tell you about their band performance, wrestling match, crazy mother, broken heart, temptation, struggles, and triumphs. By the way, I don't approve of high school wrestling. I'll probably preach about that eventually, but, at the youth event, I'm just listening.

Keep them out partying until *they're* ready to go home. Don't talk about how tired you are, how early you have to get up, or how hard you've had to work. Don't tell them how small your salary is, or that there is no salary at all. You're laying up paychecks in heaven. They may never really appreciate what we're doing for them. That's okay. It's not about us anyway. I want them to know that I *LOVE* youth events and I can't wait for the next one because I love them. You may have to sleep until noon Friday to prepare, or until three on Saturday to recover. It's all a part of the job.

Love Them With Your Patience

Don't be irritable. Let them scream in the van, run wild, cheat at the games, and say stupid things. Smile at them. Laugh at them. Participate with them. With your eyes, tell each one of them that they are truly extraordinary. Don't yell unless you're preaching, or they're about to walk out in front of a train—true story. Reason with them the way you'd like your boss to talk to you. And, when they don't get it, understand that they are fourteen years old and sky-high on hormones. You couldn't pay me to be a teen again. It's the hardest thing most of us have ever done. Don't forget that.

Forgive them when they fail. Restore them. Fight for them. Exhibit the mercy of God.

Love Them With Your Kindness

Compliment their clothes. Ask them if they've lost weight. Listen intently, looking into their eyes, when they talk. Ask them questions about their lives and activities. Let them win the game, and make sure they don't know it. Congratulate them when they win the game, and you didn't let them. Be proud of their accomplishments. Correct them in private (without breaking morality and safety protocols of course). Praise them openly. When they don't have any money, pay for their food and make sure nobody in the group knows about it. Don't let them get away with skipping youth events because they're broke. Let them make fun of your physical appearance, unless they are being purposefully disrespectful. That's another issue. But challenge it privately.

Love Them With Your Faith

Believe in your students when they don't believe in themselves. Expect and demand high standards and great achievements. Although you are patient, don't treat their failures as "just the kind of thing you were expecting." Forgive when they let you down. But, don't lower the bar. This isn't the next generation of high school dropouts and divorcees. These are the kids, "upon whom the ends of the world are come" (I Corinthians 10:11).

Teenagers can pray. They can read the Word, fast, win souls, love the lost, pay their tithes, give to missions, clean the youth room, be faithful to church, and abstain from fornication. Michael Phelps is said to have practiced swimming six hours a day as a teenager. While I consider that extreme, it illustrates a point: Teenagers are willing to make great sacrifices for whatever they are committed to. Attach your students' passions to the kingdom.

Love Them Through Preaching

Passionate, biblical, Spirit-lead preaching is "...quick, and powerful, and sharper than any twoedged sword, piercing even to the dividing asunder of soul and spirit, and of the joints and marrow, and is a discerner of the thoughts and intents of the heart" (Hebrews 4:12).

The world is an abrasive carnal force, causing calluses on the hearts of our students. They desperately need the power of the preached Word to stimulate their consciences to repentance. Preach to them. Prepare yourself through prayer, Bible study, and fasting. Then, study the art of preaching. Listen to old tapes and watch Pentecostal sermons online. Accept criticism from your pastor. Learn how to communicate the Word through pulpit ministry. After you have earned their respect by becoming the person God called you to be, use it to preach the truth to them.

Preach with passion. Study. Learn to preach with little or no notes. Learn how to give an altar call and help create an environment of prayer.

Love is not some dripping cliché, nor is it an action to be accomplished in a moment. Love is a commitment to being and to doing. Love compels us to be the man or woman God needs us to be. Love also compels us to give and behave sacrificially, day in and day out, for as long as we must. Loving our neighbor, that second of Great Commandments, is antithetical to carnal passions. It is truly a countercultural characteristic that will draw students to Christ and motivate them to take up their own cross and follow Him.

14 - Rules of Engagement

Give, give again, and give some more. Love until it hurts. Forgive and preach until you don't have anything left. However, never allow your passion and good intentions—for an individual or the group—to cause you to compromise good principles. Never lose sight of your calling, or let go of your judgment, no matter how compelling or desperate the situation is. Don't stop breathing so they can have breath. If your ministry dies, it is lost to all those in this group who God depends on you to reach. The extenuating situation that calls on you to compromise just this once, is almost never life or eternity threatening, or anywhere near how serious it presents itself to be. Even if it is, it still doesn't justify abandoning good practices. Always do what's right ... always.

Scenario One

> She's a 15-year-old girl you've known since she was born. She is beautiful, talented, and smart. She has fallen into sin or is in danger of doing so. She may be pregnant or she could get pregnant if things don't change. You're the first person she's confided in. She is there in your office, she is crying, she's broken, and she needs a comforting embrace. She wants to make you her tower of strength. She could be suicidal. She seems to be at a breaking point.

A caring embrace might make her feel better. Although every ounce of good sense you have says don't go here, your paternal instincts, or maybe something a little less noble, are crying out for a waiver from principles just this one time.

There's only one right thing to do in this moment: **RUN, RUN, RUN, RUN, RUN, RUN!!!!!!!!**

But what if she kills herself? Run … and call her parents, or 911 if it makes you feel better. But what if she backslides? Run … her walk with God is between her and God. What if she does get pregnant? Run … it's not the first time one of God's precious children got pregnant out of wedlock. God can forgive her and give her a second chance.

What if she has an abortion? Run … again, this is between her and God.

You falling into sin isn't going to help her.

You going to jail isn't going to help her.

You being falsely accused of sin isn't going to help her.

You feeling less than completely ethical isn't going to help her.

Giving a place for the enemy to temp you isn't going to help her.

And, if you fail now, when she does try to get back right with God, what use will you be to her then?

General Principles

- Never counsel a member of the opposite sex alone.
- Never be in a room alone with the opposite sex.
- Never be alone in a vehicle with a member of the opposite sex.
- Never allow yourself to usurp the role of the Savior.
- Never allow fear to motivate rash decisions.
- Bring parents in on their children's secrets.
- Never keep secrets of the opposite sex by yourself—make sure your wife or a qualified third party is involved.
- Always seek counsel from your pastor if you find yourself in a potentially compromising situation.
- Pray for this girl every day.
- If you are tempted, run.
- When in doubt, run.

Scenario Two

He's sixteen years old. He's athletic, has a photographic memory—only with lines from comedies—and he's sincere. He is adopted but seems to be well adapted. He is faithful to everything you do and helps with anything you ask. He is a committed Christian, his parents are not so committed members of the church. They seem to facilitate anything stupid or sinful he wants to do, and they balk at every good decision. He is angry at his parents and has often vented his frustration to you. He wants to attend Bible college, but his parents strongly disagree. They have given him an ultimatum, either drop the notion of Bible college or you're grounded, from everything. His parents are wrong, but his spirit is too. He wants to move in with you so that he can avoid the repercussions of his decision to pursue what he feels like is God's will.

In our pride it is easy to trump the authority of parents. However, we have no biblical precedent to do so. How can we teach them to honor their father and mother if we indulge their rebellion? How can they have the blessings of God if they are in rebellion?

The answer: Seek counsel from your pastor, and in the meantime, honor parents.

But what if he just moves in with someone from his school and backslides? That's between him and God. Everybody has to choose.

But what if he goes to the university his parents are pushing and he gets lost in the process? Am I not somewhat to blame? Absolutely not.

What if he is angry and hurt by my refusal and rejects me and the church? God is well aware of the situation and has the power to do a miracle. God is working on that right now. You compromising Scripture to work things out is not a part of God's plan.

General Principles

- Respect the parents of your students.
- Refuse to be a part of a student's disrespect and rebellion.
- Never take sides with a student against parents.

- Don't overstep your bounds of authority.
- Don't overestimate your wisdom or power to help.
- Pray for this young man and his parents daily.
- Seek council from your pastor.
- Never neglect the needs or safety of your own children by taking someone into your home.

Take a deep breath, get some counsel, and make good choices. With care, we can avoid the dangers. We can be the best advocates our students have.

15 - Never Stop Learning

As a general rule, throughout my ministry, many things I thought I knew turned out to be wrong. We've done some other things, purely by accident that turned out to be right. All said, ministry has been a very humbling experience for me. In addition to practicing spiritual disciplines, we have to keep learning.

Read

It doesn't give me any pleasure to tell you about the attitude I had during my Bible college years. In class one morning, the professor was going around the room asking each student where they got their inspiration to preach. Many shared different books they had read. Others referenced sermon tapes. They talked about special book trips and how to build a library. When the teacher got to me, I said, "I get my inspiration from my head." Yep! That's what I said. Even worse, I meant it.

I was a year or so into my ministry when my inspiration dried up. Who knew that what I thought was an artesian aquifer turned out to be stagnant pool an inch deep. Unbelievably, it would be many years before I really made the commitment to finding a new well.

"I hate to read," and "I'm a terrible reader." These were the statements that helped keep me in ignorance. My father is a notable author of several great books. My personal favorite is *"They Came to Save Us."* It was during one of my father's book-signings in Indianapolis, Indiana that everything began to change. I picked up a book by Audie Murphy, entitled *"To Hell and Back."* I couldn't put the book down. I read it cover to cover in a couple days. After finishing the book, something occurred to me: I didn't hate to read, it was simply that I wasn't excited by much of *what* I was reading. I decided to find another book in the military memoir genre and see if I could repeat the experience. I was astounded. Not only did I not hate reading, I loved it. As my desire for reading increased, so did my range of subjects. I found that the more I read, the more I wanted to read. I developed an appetite for a wide range of subjects from language to politics.

I began setting annual reading goals, and achieving them. A good friend and I began challenging each other for more motivation. My first year I read as many books as I had read in the previous decade. My goals have increased every year.

Reading is an integral part of my life. Along with Scripture and prayer, reading is a constant spring of information and inspiration, motivating, convicting, and teaching me.

WWW.Audible.com is a tool that has helped me tremendously. These days I listen to most of my books, and I love it even more. I read much like I pray; when I can. I read or listen to books when I'm waiting on an appointment, driving, or while my wife is shopping. I take in thirty minutes to an hour each night before bed.

Here's a brief essay on the topic:

A fool believes he knows it all and proudly attempts to illustrate as much. An unlimited ocean of words is produced from a stagnant pool. This level of ignorance is to be avoided at all cost. For the novice, knowledge slows speaking, but impulsive words flow from a trickle of information. Indulge the ramblings of the partially educated at your own risk. For the persevering student, learning and talking must eventually come to a draw. A stream of words will flow from a stream of information. There's hope for the one who can listen as much as they want to be heard. Reading, listening, and a desire to know stanches the monologue. A trickle of words flows from a river of information. Don't mistake silence for ignorance, acquiescence, or approval. If you want the opinion of a learner, you may have to solicit it. I've observed the wise. I envy their capacity to learn and propensity to forbear. Sparse words fitly spoken flow from an ocean of information. If an erudite speaks, wise men listen.

Don't Be Afraid Of Advice

Insecurity can make us commit a couple of different errors. We may abandon great ideas because someone suggests something different, or we may reject them outright by course, rather than reason. Insecurity has no place in youth ministry. If your plan is working, don't let people lead you away from success. However, don't automatically reject ideas just because they aren't yours. Learn from others. Listening is a rare art.

Longevity

There is good news. If you will keep learning, in time, you will get very good at this. Stick with it. Through Bible Study and prayer, reading, and listening, you will develop into a minister whose leadership is irresistible. Countercultural leaders compel by their lives and passion, rarely by their demands.

Section Two
Making Youth Ministry A Reality

16 - The 80/20 Principle

According to Richard Koch, "The 80/20 Principle," in the world there is a "profound imbalance in how the spoils are divided."[6] In 1897 Vilfredo Pareto noticed the phenomenon which is widely referred to today as "the 80/20 Principle." It is "based around the rough observation that the top twenty percent of any distribution usually accounts for about eighty percent of its power or impact."[7] Koch writes, "In business, many studies have shown that the most popular twenty percent of products account for approximately eighty percent of sales; and that the twenty percent of the largest customers also account for about eighty percent of sales; and that roughly twenty percent of sales account for eighty percent of profits. Likewise, it is a safe bet that about eighty percent of crime will be accounted for by only twenty percent of criminals, that eighty percent of accidents will be due to twenty percent of drivers, that eighty percent of wear and tear on your carpets will occur in only twenty percent of their area, and that twenty percent of your clothes get worn eighty percent of the time."[8]

Assuming the Pareto's rule is true, we have to ask, what is the twenty percent of what we do that will result in eighty percent of the results? Also, flipping the rule upside down, we have to inquire: What is the eighty percent of things I do in ministry that will only account for twenty percent of desired outcome?

If we had unlimited time and resources, these questions wouldn't be as important. But I'm forty-one years old. I have to make every moment count. Once we establish what the twenty percent is, we have to take aim like an archer, releasing time and recourses at the same target over and over again. In the next chapters I will discuss the three elements I have identified as that twenty percent.

---

[6] Koch, Richard (2014-04-15). The 80/20 Principle and 92 Other Powerful Laws of Nature: The Science of Success (Kindle Location 3635). Nicholas Brealey Publishing. Kindle Edition.
[7] Ibid
[8] Ibid

17 - Developing Your Core

David had his mighty men. Jesus had His twelve. Actually, Jesus had the twelve, and then He had Peter, James, and John. While Jesus did not neglect the crowd, He had an incrementally narrowed group of men in His inner-circle or "core." These men received exclusive time and teaching from the master, and, it was these men that would spearhead revival across the world. Who are the "core" people in your ministry who are receiving your focused attention and helping fight the fight and spread the Word?

We will be with everyone at youth events. We teach the crowd. In addition, we should have a smaller group of specific individuals that get more attention. Jesus said, "… I pray not for the world, but for them which thou hast given me" (John 17:9).

Developing Your Leadership Core

Depending on the size of your church, there are potentially dozens or more people who can help with youth ministry. They will be chaperones, van drivers, event coordinators, teachers, and more. It is advantageous to you and to your group to have help from adults in the church.

Identify Potential Leaders

Look for people that are:
- Busy
- Successful
- Consistent
- Married (if possible). If they're single, make sure they're not scanning the youth group for a potential mate.
- Prayerful
- Faithful to church
- Often around the altar
- Patient
- Principled
- Willing to follow rules and directives

Often, when looking for help with youth ministry, the criteria we look for is quite different: young, trendy, lots of time, naturally enjoys hanging out with teenagers, energetic, crazy. In fact, we're looking for adults that act like teenagers. While that may seem like fun for the kids, on further review, it may not be wise. Sometimes the surface attributes that cause us to use certain people are the same qualities that disqualify them for youth ministry. Remember that we're trying to inspire teens to be Christ-like. Your leaders should mirror the same pattern that you set for yourself.

Pursue

Once you have chosen people that you feel would be an asset to your group, pursue them. Create a list of the people you want to involve.
- Introduce that list to your pastor - It is possible that he will eliminate people from your list due to circumstances that only he knows.
- Make contact - Use whatever means you're most comfortable with. Keep in mind that you should treat the pursuit of potential leaders as critical for your group. Be professional. Give the impression that this really matters to you and to the kingdom. I prefer a well-prepared letter that explains,

in detail, why I would like them to help and what I would want them to do. I ask them to contact me, perhaps with an included self addressed and stamped envelop. Few people will ignore the protocol of responding to that kind of communication.

Meet

When you feel good about a group that has agreed to be a part of your youth ministry staff, it's time to meet. Establish a date that works for the majority of the group. Suggestions for meeting:
- Rent a meeting place away from the church such as a hotel conference room or a restaurant meeting room.
- Have a meeting agenda.
- Start and end on time.
- Treat the group with great respect.
- Express your burden in brief opening statements.
- Use well-designed handouts and PowerPoint.
- Give out calendars with pre-established dates for each leader. People rarely plan their personal calendars a year in advance. If you try to get them to give you dates in advance, or before your calendar is published it may never get done. They can work out the details of their calendars later.
- Establish ground-rules for working with teens.
- Pray together.

Cultivate

Spend time with leaders, going to dinner, engaging in recreation, or meeting over coffee. Let them see and hear your heartbeat. Remind them of the value of their commitments to the young people. Pray for them every day.

Leaders who prove themselves to be principled and faithful are a great asset to your students. Allow them to be an influence. Allow them to have relationships with the group. Allow their talents to shine in ministry. Fight the temptation to limit their access to teens because of your jealousy or insecurity. If they can preach, let them.

If they preach better than you, you are blessed to have them. If they are fun and connect well with teens, encourage these relationships. Don't allow "smallness" to make you territorial. Your ministry will not be hindered by great "core" leaders; rather, it will be enhanced exponentially. Embrace great leadership. Jesus never intended to reach the world on His own. Neither should you, or can you. He was God. Identifying, pursuing, and cultivating great leadership is definitely part of the twenty percent that will result in high yield.

Developing Your Youth Core

In most groups you will have teens that naturally gravitate to you. You don't choose them, rather, they choose that role for themselves. It isn't an exclusive club that you elect. Anyone can be in the core. In fact, your ultimate goal is that your entire group would.

This core is defined by their faithfulness to events, commitment to the principles you teach, and passion to be involved. Mentor these students with your words and your example. Allow them to see Christ through you.

Let me throw in a quick caveat. Don't show open favoritism to the core. Work to create an environment of fairness. The last thing you want is animosity towards the 20%, the disciples, the mighty men. Don't allow them to influence activities or eating choices. Don't allow them to monopolize your time or attention when you are with the group. They may try to do this because they are young and immature. Hold them at bay, for their own good and for the good of the group. This is very hard to do, but it's necessary.

Teach them as much as they will let you. Inspire them to pray, to read the Word, fast, and live a moral lifestyle. Teach them to live counterculturally. You're not trying to attract them to yourself. Use any emotional or spiritual capital you have with them to challenge them to be more like Christ. You aren't the deliverer. Don't allow yourself to be a surrogate Savior. You don't want codependent students. You want liberated disciples of Jesus.

As the core gets closer to the cross, the *cross* will transform them like it did Stephen in Acts chapter six. Imagine a series of concentric circles with Jesus in the middle. Your core is nearest to the center. As the core moves towards the cross, their influence reaches to the next circle and pulls them closer to the center. That group's lifestyle is magnetic to the next group, and so on. Sometimes this is less about superior spirituality and more about their age. Those that have been in the group a while may very well be closer than those that are new. Depending on your leadership, the longer the older ones are there, the closer they will get to Christ. Newer students will observe the lives of their predecessors and be drawn to similar commitments. In explaining the countercultural phenomenon of the sixties, Roszak writes, "On the major campuses, it is often enough the graduates who assume positions of leadership.... The role of these campus elders is crucial."

Like Christ, you must love, teach, lead, preach, and fellowship with the whole group, and to the youth of the community at large. You must also, like Jesus, develop the core of your ministry so they can aid you and your leadership team in the work of the Lord. The core will develop relationships with others in the group and in their circle of influence in their families, schools, and places of employment. They will go where you can't go. They will multiply your influence and magnify the message. This effect is heightened as your tenure increases.

18 - The Scooby-Doo Principle

I have my own rule: the Scooby-Doo principle. Okay, I admit it doesn't sound as cool as the Pareto Rule, but it's bound to be a classic. Anyone who has ever seen an episode of Scooby Doo, has seen them all. Let me remind you. Theme song:

> "Scooby Dooby Doo where are you
> We've got some work to do now
> Scooby Dooby Doo
> We need some help from you now ..."

The "gang" will begin the episode by visiting family or friends in some interesting location. They will drive in their hippie-van, eat lots of food, and get scared a lot. There will be at least one chase scene where, at some point, Scooby will get some "Scooby-Snacks," at which point he will find his courage. There will be a ghost, monster, or some other villain which will turn out to be some guy/girl, probably a museum curator or the like. The perpetrator will be unmasked by the end of the episode and say, "And I would have gotten away with it too if it weren't for you meddling kids." The plot is so predictable that its predictability was part of the plot. The "gang" even corrected the villain if they didn't say the right line when they were revealed. Hollywood geniuses followed suit with shows like

Blue's Clues and *Dora the Explorer*. "I'm the map, I'm the map, I'm the map, et cetera..." "We're gonna think, think..." You remember. And, that is the point. As bad as you hate *Blue Clues*, if you have a child, the basics of the show are seared into your consciousness for as long as you live on this planet. Which makes me mad.

How do we sear the most important things into the lives of our students? We teach and/or preach them over, and over, and over until they are reciting them in their sleep. Like another unimaginative episode of the classic cartoons, we role it out every week... until the end of time.

What are the things? The answer to that question is so simple as to sound like a Sunday School cliché, and complicated enough that the answer doesn't seem like a clarification. The things are the principles found in Scripture. I can almost hear your sigh of annoyance while I'm writing this. You're probably saying, "Duh, thank you for that, Captain Obvious." I know, and I'm sorry, but it's just that simple and complex. So what now?

Putting Out Fires

Where did you hear the sermons that most impacted your life? What services stand out to you as the most profound? If you're anything like me, it was a conference, a camp, or maybe a youth convention. At these kinds of venues, organizations role out the nation's greatest communicators to create experiences that will impact the lives of teens for years to come. These events happen annually or more infrequently. They often address key subjects that have been predetermined by committees that may even follow a conference/camp theme. They typically employ topical preaching. Topical preaching is powerful and useful. I'm not suggesting that we shouldn't employ it. However, topical preaching tends to "put out fires," rather than putting "...precept upon precept; line upon line, line upon line; here a little, and there a little" (Isaiah 28:10). These events are invaluable for inspiration and conviction. However, their format is not, in itself, a complete biblical diet for weekly youth ministry. It is difficult, if not impossible, in this way to present the broad range of subjects taught in Scripture. If you're asked to preach a youth camp, follow the example of your favorite preacher. But, for weekly, monthly, yearly, and generational ministry, follow the Scooby-Doo principle—a.k.a. expository preaching and teaching. This is teaching the simple, plain, seemingly mundane subjects of Scripture over and over again.

I was a fire putter-outer preacher for many years. My conversion came hard. There was a young woman in our youth group who seemed to really get it. She was involved with everything: singing, playing, working in the church. She always responded appropriately to my topical sermons. I thought it was enough. I didn't know otherwise until a wind of false doctrine blew through her family. I never would have believed that she would be led away from truth so quickly. With great regret, too late, I realized that I had given her too much of my words and not enough of the Word. My passionate sermons cannot replace the God-breathed inspiration of Scripture. I wouldn't need to be taught this lesson twice. I immediately restructured our entire teaching program around systematic, weekly reading of Scripture by the whole group, and systematic teaching of the chapters we had read during the week.

Expository Preaching/Teaching

According to the infamous Wikipedia, "Expository preaching is a form of preaching that details the meaning of a particular text or passage of Scripture. It explains what the Bible means by what it says." What are we going to teach? We are going to teach exactly what the Bible says.

For us, expository teaching starts with Bible reading assignments. We will discuss that in a later chapter.

Next, we teach as many of the chapters as we can, going verse by verse. Frequently, students engage with questions and comments they have formulated while reading throughout the week. I have never experienced a more exciting format for discovering and teaching.

Advantages Of Expository Teaching/Preaching

1 - We are forced to declare the whole Council of God

Paul declares himself to be, "...pure from the blood of all men. For I have not shunned to declare unto you all the counsel of God" (Acts 20:26 - 27). By teaching the Scriptures methodically we are saying what God wanted to say rather than picking topics and looking for corroborating Scripture. "Thy Word" David said, "have I hid in my heart." The Word of God is "quick and powerful" and "living." It's God's Word that is going to nourish students' hearts and minds.

2 - We're forced to teach hot topics

Frankly, there's some stuff I don't like teaching about. For example, I don't enjoy talking about money or sex. The problem is, God talks about finances and sexual purity too frequently to be ignored. While my topical sermons may never venture into this unfriendly territory, God's Word goes there without hesitation. By teaching through the Scriptures I am more likely not to miss important stuff subconsciously because it's uncomfortable to talk about.

3 - We can teach with impunity

Have you ever been guilty of preaching on Sunday against sins that you discovered your students were committing on Friday? That's a great way to make enemies. More likely, you have been tempted *not* to preach something Sunday because you were afraid it would look like you were doing it spitefully. By systematically going through planned books of the Bible and specific chapters, you are forced to teach even when you might have put it off, and you have impunity from suspicion of being vindictive. Everyone knew since January what you were going to teach in October. "I sure wasn't picking on your child. That lesson was on the calendar six months before your child did that."

Follow the Scooby-Doo principle. Preach what Scripture says, exactly what it says, over, and over, and over. Everything it talks about, you talk about. Everything it condemns, you condemn. Everything it commands, you command. In doing so, we are freed from following poplar topical currents. We are untethered from political-correctness and forced to disavow our personal soapboxes. We are, in fact, teaching the "whole council of God."

You may be tempted to rush or skip over what seems obvious or old-hat to you. Be careful. In teaching the actual Scriptures you are going to be redundant, because God, apparently, is redundant. It may very well get boring to you. Remember, however, in most cases, you have been studying Scripture much longer than they have. What is common-knowledge to you may be new for them. You don't need to give them something new. You need to preach the old stuff until it is as familiar as "… if it hadn't been for you meddling kids." Phrases like, "Here oh Israel the Lord our God is one," "pray without ceasing," and "Repent, and be baptized every one of you in the name of Jesus Christ for the remission of sins," ought to be second nature to your students.

I am convinced that the greatest threat to the church in the twenty-first century is a lack of Bible knowledge. There are millions of people in North America alone who are certain that they are on their way to heaven but can't quote one Scripture in its proper context that substantiates their claims. They can tell you what they believe, or what a television preacher said. They can even quote modern religious literature about heaven, love, or prosperity, but they don't have any idea what the Bible says about how to be saved or how to live. This is a tragic reality and a marvelous opportunity. "In the land of the blind, the one-eyed man is king." Teach your students what the Bible says. If they will even half-listen, they will be a countercultural force in this world. With just a basic understanding of Scripture they could point their world to a Savior that was lifted up on a cross and the power of that truth "will draw all men" unto Him.

19- Involve Youth in Real Ministry

I was pretty sure it was going to be the worst youth event ever. For some reason that I can't now recall, someone had suggested that the youth group visit our church shut-ins. I'm not sure how, but that terrible idea made it onto our calendar.

The plan was to take a group of over thirty teenagers to several of the homes of our elderly saints. We would sing, testify, pray, give them gifts and be on our way. I planned to try to repay our teens who would surely hate this night, with something more fun later on.

First, we stopped by Walmart and picked up some crossword puzzle books, fuzzy slippers, and sugar-free candy. We made nice gift baskets and headed out the door to kick off the disaster. What happened next was shocking.

The kids sang like they meant it. They were respectful in small, and sometimes filthy, homes. They touched the aging men and women we visited, even hugging them. There were many tears, some from those we visited and some from teenagers. It turned out to be one the best events we have ever had, so we made it an annual event. Through the years, groups of young people have found great joy in visiting people who are the embodied opposite of everything youthful. Through this, and other experiences, I've learned something philosophical about teens as well as practical about youth ministry.

First, the philosophy. As much as teens seem to be selfish, there is something in them that wants to give. They don't just want to hear sermons, be evangelized, or watch an offering being taken. They want to preach, reach, and give.

Are we surprised by this? What kid wants to watch the ballgame from the bench? By nature we aren't only spectators, we are participators. If we'll let them onto the floor, they will keep coming to the games. Kids want to feel like they have a purpose.

I have learned that whether it be a youth event, a service, a class, or another ministry, the kids that might not sit quiet for a ten minute lesson will behave perfectly if they have a purpose. Students who never give back can develop a selfish mentality. They show up saying, "whatcha gonna do for me tonight?" Hands-on-ministry taps into a better part of a teenager's nature.

Second, the practical blessing. Teenagers are some of the most talented people I know. They can do great things in the Kingdom. Remember Josiah? "Josiah was eight years old when he began to reign... in the eighth year of his reign, while he was yet young, he began to seek after the God of David his father: and in the twelfth year he began to purge Judah and Jerusalem from the high places, and the groves, and the carved images, and the molten images" (2 Chronicles 34:1-3). Teens can help pray and fast, win the lost, lead in music and worship, preach, teach, work, and give.

Involve Them In Praying And Fasting

Some don't believe that it is practical to expect teenagers to make substantial prayer commitments. In the book, "Reaching a Generation for Christ," it states, "I can recall a junior high retreat where I encouraged students to make a commitment to pray for thirty minutes a day when they returned home. In a desire to please God and their youth pastor, they made the commitment. I felt very satisfied about the results until about Wednesday of the week after the retreat. As I began to reflect on how much difficulty I was having in keeping that commitment, I repented for what I had done to those students in my sincere, but misguided, zeal. I had set the students up for failure in their attempts to develop a spiritual discipline. What seemed to be a good idea was actually a bad one."⁹

Let me get this right; It's a bad idea to ask teens to make a commitment to prayer? I won't rehash the value of prayer in our kids' lives. I think they are perfectly capable even if it was just a value-less Christian discipline. If sixteen-year-old Josiah can take a stand against the power of idolatry in Judah and Jerusalem, my young people can make sincere and powerful commitments in prayer. Does that mean they'll be perfect in keeping all commitments? No, but "Where there is no vision, the people perish" (Proverbs 29:18). Live a high standard and call them to join you. They will.

It makes me sick that millions of teens, who are on their way to hell, make incredible sacrifices to be a part of a counter or sub-culture. They willingly allow multiple piercings, bars, and gauges to be inflicted upon their bodies. They are tattooed, even on the face. They give up social acceptance, affluence, and comfort to identify with something that has no lasting value. Other teens pour themselves into activities that have carnal benefits, but no eternal consequence. Athletes will work out and train for hours a day. Musicians will practice while friends are partying, because they have a dream. Seventeen year olds gain parental approval to sign away their lives to the military. But, Christian teenagers can't be asked to pray because it might offend their delicate constitutions? Are you kidding me? "And others had trial of cruel mockings and scourgings, yea, moreover of bonds and imprisonment: They were stoned, they were sawn asunder, were tempted, were slain with the sword: they wandered about in sheepskins and goatskins; being destitute, afflicted, tormented; (Of whom the world was not worthy:) they wandered in deserts, and in mountains, and in dens and caves of the earth. And these all, having obtained a good report through faith, received not the promise" (Hebrews 11:36-39).

Introduce a great need or vision to your youth group. Ask students to pray and fast for a miracle. They will be inspired as they deny themselves for a great cause. I've seen it happen. And what will move the heart of God like a thirteen-year-old girl who has the faith to rebel against self-gratification through prayer and fasting? Don't tell my teens they can't be prayer warriors. "But Jesus said, Suffer little children, and forbid them not, to come unto me: for of such is the kingdom of heaven" (Matthew 19:14).

Most teens don't like two-hand-touch, scoreless games, winner-less matches, or tepid pronouncements that *everyone is* a winner. Neither do they want a church that does not call them to action.

Our Christian school has been without a building for eleven weeks of the current school year. They have been having classes in a gymnasium awaiting state approval to occupy a property we purchased months ago. After waiting for quite some time, only two days ago we received another very discouraging communiqué from the state. We learned that the process had not even started yet, and they were blaming us. The ordeal was set to drag out another six weeks or more. While all this has been going on, our high school students have been reading *"The Circle Maker,"* by Mark Batterson. I highly recommend the book. Some of those students decided to follow Batterson's advice to "pray circles around your need." Two days ago, as of this writing, several students went to our new campus and walked around it, claiming it in prayer. Another group went this very day and repeated the act of faith. Within three hours of that prayer meeting, at 4:45 PM this afternoon, what our architect firm called "a miracle" transpired. Within twenty-four hours of receiving our new application, the request was granted. I am convinced that a group of teens prayed in faith and God responded. There are several teens who believe the same thing. They will use that faith to engage greater challenges in the future.

Involve Them In Outreach

We started a Saturday outreach program that was staffed by teens from twelve to eighteen years old. They worked with underprivileged and often foul smelling and wild children from our community. They transported the kids to our facility, cooked for them, played games with them, lead them in worship, and taught them a Bible lesson. Although this ministry has been discontinued due to students graduating and making other ministry commitments, some of the kids they reached are still in the church today.

The commitments of our students in this ministry awed me. On one occasion, a slightly irritated grandma came to me asking that I would *force* her granddaughter to spend the day with her. Although she loved her grandma, she would not miss even a single outreach event on a Saturday. Another student asked her family to postpone a vacation that was in honor of her birthday. The scheduled get-away would have caused her to miss outreach. I'll never forget the many hours of total sacrifice given to children that would never be able to give back. I promise you these kids will turn the world upside down.

Involve Them In Music And Worship

Many of our students are involved with music and worship. Through the years, students have formed bands that have enriched services and retreats, as well as providing inspiration to budding new musicians. Many of them have gone on to college-level praise and worship ministry as well as professional music careers.

In addition to youth ministry, I pastor a growing church in rural Indiana. For the first two years, I relied completely on teenagers for music. Like clockwork, our students met every Sunday morning for the forty-five minute drive to our church. I don't know how we would have done it without this faithful group. Today, we still have several young musicians from our youth group involved in the music ministry. Other members help with music at another church nearly an hour away from our town. Still more of our young people fill several music ministry roles at our weekly services. It's a blessing to the kids and invaluable to the ministry of our church.

It is not that our kids just have a lot of talent. It is focused training and opportunity that has made the difference. Several years ago, a previous music director told our pastor that we could not have a youth choir because the kids had no talent. Our current music director has spent more than a decade teaching piano lessons and giving teens the opportunity to be involved with music. This has made all the difference. If you don't currently have teens ready to take part in music and worship, plan for the long-term. Encourage students to get lessons, or, even better, provide a teacher.

Encourage Them To Preach

Give them an opportunity to preach. If there isn't a venue for it, create one.

I don't recommend giving a rookie a thirty minute slot to fill. It's overwhelming and sets them up for failure. First, create an atmosphere that *anyone* would like to peach in. Give them five minutes. Make sure there is music ready to start when they conclude. If they don't do it themselves, be prepared to lead the group in a time of prayer. Make sure the service doesn't fall flat. Be ready with a sermon to fill any remaining schedule. Don't leave the impression that more was expected.

Nothing is more exciting than young people who feel a call to preach. One of the greatest joys in my life is seeing our kids enter into a life of ministry.

Help Them Teach, Work, And Give

Involve them in teaching Sunday School, children's church, or a children's choir. Give them the chance to clean, decorate, build, or do other work projects. Inspire them to pay their tithes, give to church needs and charities, and support missionaries around the world.

As your students dedicate themselves to God's work in new ways, they will become inseparably tied to His Kingdom. Their hearts will be invested.

A Word Of Caution

The first time I met Daniel, he was in the county jail. The methamphetamine had been gone from his system for several months. In his right mind, he wanted to be baptized. It was a joy to be a part of that occasion.

Months later, he was out of jail and on a mission. He had a great job with a reputable company in the city. He had mentors in his life and a proud family cheering him on. He was studying the Bible every day with an eye on foreign missions work.

Daniel came to me one day with exciting news. A local church had asked him to give his testimony of deliverance to their youth group. I advised him to accept the offer. The anticipated event came quickly and surpassed expectations. Our youth band led the large crowd of teens in worship before Daniel spoke. Then he took the floor and set the house ablaze with his impassioned testimony. He spoke with the conviction of a young man who has been to the brink and returned. The crowd was moved and entered into a time of prayer. Daniel's drug-free life would last approximately two more hours.

I should have seen it coming. I should have taken him to get a burger that night and talked to him about pride and temptation. I should have prayed with him and explained that some besetting sins will never fight to the death, they simply retreat and live to make war another day.

I did nothing. I said nothing. I'm partially to blame for his drug relapse. My last encounter with Daniel was in a Walmart parking lot late one night after a youth event. He was beside himself, pacing, kneeling, misquoting Scriptures, and talking nonsense under the influence of drugs. After an hour of feeling awkward I finally came to my senses. I challenged the young man I once knew, and asked, "Is this what you really want?" My boldness came far too late to reach him.

You are responsible to help prepare teens for the challenges they will face once involved with ministry. First, teach them to pray. I heard someone say that they don't want to pray too much, because they don't want to be on the front line of the battle. They felt like it was safer to keep a low profile in the spirit. That is utter nonsense. Everyone is in a battle. Prayer does not make you more vulnerable to attack; rather, it gives you insight into the battle that is already raging, and it equips you to engage successfully. Doing ministry without prayer is like hearing the sounds of battle and charging to the front-line blind and weaponless.

Encourage kids to "pray without ceasing." Do not put them in a position of any kind of ministry unless they are praying. Pray *for* them. Talk to them about pride and temptation. Teach them that ministry is never about their ego. Teach them that God will never allow anyone to glory in His presence. Teach them that ministry has to be about Christ, and Him alone. Create a forum for them to communicate with you, a parent, or another mentor about temptation. Warn them that temptations will come. In Luke 22:31-32 Jesus mentors Peter, warns him about sin, and informs him that He is praying for him. Again, in Matthew 26, Jesus admonishes Peter to pray because of a coming storm of temptation.

Use kids in ministry, but be diligent in prayer and mentoring so that you aren't setting students up for a very hard fall. For, "…the spirit indeed is willing, but the flesh is weak" (Matthew 26:41).

---

[9](1997-03-05). Reaching a Generation for Christ: A Comprehensive Guide to Youth Ministry (Kindle Locations 739-744). Moody Publishers. Kindle Edition.

20 - Winning New Students

Outreach is one of the clearest scriptural mandates, and one of the hardest to fulfill. Most people are at least attempting to obey the Great Commission, with sometimes less than the desired results. How do we share the gospel with the world in a way that compels them to come in?

Don't Lose The Core

I've seen churches that focused almost solely on evangelism to the exclusion of worship, fellowship, Bible teaching, and other parts of ministry. I recall one church that poured almost all of its financial recourses, man-power, and time into busing children to church. The program was extremely successful at bringing large numbers of children to Sunday School, and it was certainly a worthy endeavor. However, in time, the neglect of essential parts of ministry left the people burned-out. Most of the children who were brought to church did not make lasting commitments to God. And many of the adults that had given so much of their lives to reaching lost children were eventually lost themselves.

It is natural to feel a great compassion towards the lost, and especially children or people in dire circumstances. However, soothing our aching consciences by throwing lots of energy and money towards people who are hurting does not automatically satisfy the Great Commission. It's crucial that we actually "make disciples." If we aren't focused on biblical evangelism we may abandon good practices and go running after students, with a net gain of very little positive results, and even some negative. Yes, Jesus taught us about His unfailing love through the parable of leaving the ninety-nine in search of the one. However, Jesus is also the one who spent most of His time with twelve men, and often just three. He's also the one who said He didn't pray for the world, but for a specific few that had been given to Him. Jesus' primary method of evangelism was the discipling of men who then discipled others.

We are called to love. You should be teaching your own home Bible study out of love for the lost and as an example. However, we can't neglect the core. We can't just put together large venue events and expect the world to come running to God.

Consider these statistics which show the primary reason why people come to church:

2% by Advertisement
6% by the Pastoral Invitation
6% by organized evangelism campaign
86% by friends or relatives[10]

Here is our ten-step formula for winning the lost:

1 - Continue the process of "becoming" the countercultural leader God has called you to be.
2 - Teach and preach the Word.
3 - Inspire students to live a countercultural Christian life through faithfulness, prayer, fasting, and Bible study.
4 - Give ample amounts of your time to students that gravitate towards God.
5 - Make living for God exciting and fun.
6 - As students draw closer to God with enthusiasm, other students will be drawn to that end. These other students will be those that have not been as faithful or passionate as well as children who have graduated from the Sunday School department into your youth group.

7 - As the entire group becomes more Christ-like, the love of God working in them will connect with unchurched students in their circles of influence (friends, family, acquaintances).

8 - Your students can teach biblical principles by example and through a one-on-one Bible study.

9 - Your students can invite these people to godly youth events where they will build relationships with your group, then to classes where they will begin to learn Bible doctrine, and ultimately to services where they will experience the saving power of God's Spirit.

10 - One or two at a time, new converts will become assimilated into a Christ-like group, eventually becoming counter-cultural themselves.

Don't Get Impatient

Some feel very frustrated or even guilty because they aren't winning the lost fast enough. Our impatience can cause us to neglect what we should be doing, to engage in practices that we hope will expedite the process. Well intentioned people reference the huge revival crusade that took place in Acts 2 as a blueprint for how modern revival should look. Lets imagine just that sort of scenario:

We rent an auditorium in the city. We pray and fast for a week, asking God to pour out His Spirit. We purchase ad-space in local newspapers and on television and radio stations. We rent a billboard and create matching flyers to hand out to local junior high and high school students. We hire a recognizable Christian band and a speaker who excels at communicating with teens. We pack out the auditorium, but the crowd feels disproportionately weighted towards Christian people who came to hear the band. The music group is amazing, except for their less than desirable clothes, hairdos, ecumenical philosophy, and "Jacksonian" dance moves. The speaker calls kids to make a commitment to Christ. Most of the seekers seem to be members of other churches. The suspicion is substantiated when none of them show up for our highly publicized Sunday morning service. Giving away prizes doesn't even help. We spent seven thousand dollars, months of planning, and incalculable amounts of faith-capital, not to make disciples, but only to make an impression. And, not necessarily a good one.

Why can't we see three thousand souls added to our youth group in one day? Why can't we see three-hundred, or even three real conversions with a scenario like that? While there are some large events that make more than an impression on a community, more often than not, this isn't the case. The simple answer is this: you will probably not have an Acts 2 revival in your community. Now, before you pronounce me to be a faithless heretic and go burn this book, let me explain why that is okay, and even good news.

First, lets consider the monologue that Jesus shares in John 4. We often quote verse 35, "Behold, I say unto you, Lift up your eyes, and look on the fields; for they are white already to harvest." This is exciting news. The problem is, we claim that part of the passage, shut our Bibles, and call to book our auditorium, without reading the rest of the text. Jesus explains why these particular fields are "white" in verse 38, "I sent you to reap that whereon ye bestowed no labour: other men laboured, and ye are entered into their labours." If they were just gathering in ripe crops, who are the "men" who "labored" before them? John the Baptist is one. John, whom Jesus proclaimed was as great as any man who had ever lived, preached there for as many as three years, or more. The thanks he got was his own head on a platter. Jesus, God in flesh, would preach, heal, and perform unbelievable miracles for over three years, in addition to the reputation He had earned as a sinless child, teen, and young adult. On top of the two greatest preachers in world history, the Jews had the law of Moses for approximately fifteen-hundred years. They studied, revered, and memorized the Scriptures. When Peter referenced an obscure passage in Joel, he didn't have to take fifteen minutes explaining who Joel was. His audience was, "white unto harvest," with a very biblical world-view. Try referencing an obscure Old Testament prophet with a group of teens in this post-modern era. You'll get glassy-eyed stares from the crowd.

Not only has your community not been personally worked by Jesus in the flesh, the prophets, and John the Baptist, your field has been thoroughly salted—the practice of killing all life in good soil with devastating amounts of salt. You're reaching out to people who have a secular worldview, a tainted concept of Christ, a heretical mindset about their origin and purpose, and a distorted perspective of churches and preachers. The moral failures of television evangelists in the 80's gave way to greed, which has now become an absolute license for preachers to parade before the world, wielding "faith" and fornication without regard to their mutual exclusivity. Not only are these fields not "white," they are full of stones of false doctrine and thorns of cynicism. Before you can even start to plant what is good, you have to commit enormous amounts of work to tearing down and removing what is evil.

Perhaps, at this point, you're trying to figure out how this can possibly be good news. Here is why: by accepting the great task of redeeming undesirable fields, you are entering into fellowship with the prophets, with John the Baptist, and with Jesus Himself. As you pry up a rock, look to your left and you'll see John there prying with you. As you tear down another tangle of thorns, remember that Christ took a crown of thorn upon His head doing the very work into which you have entered. Evangelizing the world in this generation is very hard work, but you're in very good company. And of this kind of labor, the Psalmist writes, "They that sow in tears shall reap in joy. He that goeth forth and weepeth, bearing precious seed, shall doubtless come again with rejoicing, bringing his sheaves with him" (Psalms 126:5 - 6).

The key is found in Galatians 6:9, "And let us not be weary in well doing: for in due season we shall reap, if we faint not." Hang in there and do the right stuff. God will give you souls. Don't feel the pressure to perform miracles. You work the soil. You plant the seeds. You make sure the fields are getting watered. In the end God will give the increase. I'm not trying to dissuade you from dreaming of a three-thousand soul revival. I'm just saying, if that doesn't happen in your next crusade, don't be discouraged.

Neither am I trying to discourage you from having crusade-style outreach events. I think these kinds of events do well in supplementing the one-on-one work of evangelism that your students are doing. It's cool when a kid invites his friend to church and the person being invited replies, "oh yeah, I've seen something about that church." The key is to relegate mass-market evangelism to its rightful place as a "supplement" to the primary work of personal soul winning by a core group of disciples. By mass-market I mean videos, ads, flyers, mail-outs, concerts, block-parties, and the like.

Spend time with your core. Teach them to pray, study God's Word, fast, and love the lost. If they will follow your lead, you will have revival.

---

[10]Roy M. Oswald, Speed B. Leas, The Inviting Church: A Study of New Member Assimilation, (Durham, NC: Alban Institute, 1987), 44.

21 - Reaching Rebels

What is our responsibility in reaching out to church rebels? They test the rules, try our patience, and challenge our authority. How far should we go to appeal to them? As I'll share later in this chapter, I've seen entire youth programs railroaded by the will of a dissenter. I've also seen what amounted to the Ku-Klux-Klan of youth ministry, burning and hanging all but the whitest of sepulchers.

Before you proceed, it is important that you give due diligence to evaluating the individual you are dealing with. Remember that God's Word is a "discerner of the thoughts and intents of the heart" (Hebrews 4:12). We should proceed with caution when attempting to divine what perhaps only God Himself knows. Is he or she a true rebel?

Consider some alternate possibilities:

Personality Conflict?

It's less work on the front side to assume a person is bad. But, it might be little more than a personality conflict. In the long-run you may benefit greatly from something as simple as a personality test like the Myers-Briggs Type Indicator. What kind of personality do you have? What is the personality type of the people that you're having trouble with? Personality conflicts are both real and superficial. They are the source of frustration and strained relations, but they aren't necessarily the indicators of the deep seated rebellion they may insinuate. There is strength in personality diversity within your group. If you run off everybody that isn't like you, your program will end up whopper-jawed and underachieving.

Miscreant Or Misunderstood?

I've always wanted to trust my instincts about people. Often, I have relied on first-impressions to predetermine my interactions. I think I'm batting about .500. While that may get me a spot on an All-Star baseball team, it isn't an effective way to do ministry. While spiritual discernment and intuition can play a vital role in working with people, alone they are inadequate. Simply put, even at our most spiritual, we are still flawed. On occasion, my pronouncements of both virtue and vice have turned out to be shockingly wrong. Consider that the gifts of the Spirit, like tongues and interpretation, and prophesy, are balanced by Scripture and an interpreter. Should our "impressions" have a similar counterbalance? If so, what would the counterbalances be? Here are three counterbalances to help offset any preconceived impressions that may be wrong, or at best incomplete:

- The advice of a mentor (not a protégé).

- Ample time in earnest prayer (not *about* the situation, but *for* the individual … try loving them more first).

- Honest dialogue with the individual.

Good Guy, Bad Idea?

Someone said, "great people are not always good." Consider the bad decisions of some of the best people: Abraham lied, David committed adultery, and Peter denied Christ. While we're on the subject, remember some of your choices when you were sixteen. For me, that's the proverbial, "snuff-said."   On top of bad ideas, sometimes we lie about our mistakes or defend our choices. God is so patient. Stone-throwers are like the hunter-gatherers of ministry, parading around with a man-tooth-necklace, and counting coup. The days of the stone-throwers are numbered because their methods are self-defeating. We are in the people-business. Rather than casting stones, we should consider cultivating stragglers. Whether you're dealing with a pregnancy, pornography, or philandering, your patience and mercy will often reveal a student's true character. Someone said you should never judge a man before his thirtieth birthday. While I'm not sure that's a sound principle, I do know that long-suffering is worth the extra time.

While showing patient mercy is often the proper course, there are exceptions. There really are bad people in the world who have no intention of doing what is right. Naiveté and inaction, in the face of real rebellion, is irresponsible and dangerous. Remember that Winston Churchill's predecessor, Neville Chamberlain, believed he could negotiate peace with Adolph Hitler. Anthony Eden, foreign secretary of the British cabinet in 1938, approached Chamberlain with growing concerns about German rearmament. Chamberlain "refused to listen to him. 'Go home and take an aspirin,'"[11] was Chamberlain's advice. Simultaneously, Hitler is quoted as saying, "Well, two years ago when we marched into the Rhineland with a handful of battalions - at that moment I risked a great deal. If France had marched then, we should have been forced to withdraw.... but for France it is now too late!"[12] While Chamberlain considered himself wise and diplomatic, Mussolini considered England "a frightened, flabby old woman, who at the worst would only bluster and was, anyhow, incapable of making war."[13] It was this image of England that emboldened the Axis powers to move with such ferocity. While I'm not suggesting that you have a twelve-year-old Fascist on your hands, I strongly warn you not to take rebellion lightly.

Some years back, I was asked to speak at a youth retreat at an amazing venue. Upon arrival, I quickly connected with the youth pastor. His intentions were noble and his motives were sincere. He was a talented and humble guy. But, it didn't take long to see that he was in a difficult situation. He had inherited a youth group that, apparently, already had a leader. The alpha-male that was running the show was the pastor's son, and boy was he a mess. He was popular, well dressed, handsome, talented, and gifted with leadership ability. He also appeared to be a rebellious, womanizing, troublemaking, party animal who was providing pot for the students who were lucky enough to be a part of his in crowd.

It was obvious from the start that, according to him, the students could not allow God to move in their lives. The group was stifled and bound by this single rebel.

The youth pastor had made two mistakes. Rather than spending quality time with young, sincere students, he leaned towards abandoning the core to go after the rebel. Rather than building upon anything positive, he spent his energy chasing the negative. This effectively validated the rebel's supremacy. The young minister also attempted to drag the rebel to the core, obliterating what might have been an opportunity to create an example of what students should aspire to be.

Rather than accentuating the rebel, the youth pastor should have worked at minimizing his influence. You don't have to be openly aggressive or mean. Put the bulk of your time and energy into the right students. Organize events so that the guy who is an obvious threat doesn't have free reign to prey on the vulnerable. You don't have to go wolf-hunting. Just lead the sheep and watch for the predator. While you may not have power over who does what with whom throughout the week, at youth events, you create a safe environment for people who want to do what's right. Deal with open rebellion. Correct improper behavior when they exhibit it. However, don't make it your "mission" to route people out. "The servants said unto him, Wilt thou then that we go and gather them up? But he said, Nay; lest while ye gather up the tares, ye root up also the wheat with them" (Matthew 13:28 - 29).

Jesus admonishes us not to attempt to pull the rebels out of the church. However, He didn't accommodate them either. Jesus' ministry was polarizing. It so excited the passions of some followers that they would literally "take up their cross" to follow Him. Others were so enraged by his confrontational style and controversial message that they killed Him. "The father shall be divided against the son, and the son against the father; the mother against the daughter, and the daughter against the mother; the mother in law against her daughter in law, and the daughter in law against her mother in law" (Luke 12:53).

Let me ask two more questions before we put this subject to rest:

Why would your ministry create a comfortable spot for people who have no intention of living for God?

If they don't want to live for God, why would you sacrifice valuable time and resources to keep them?

Create an environment that glorifies God and rewards godly effort. Take time to mentor people who sincerely want to live for God. Minimize the influence of people who show no signs of wanting to live for God. In essence, ignore them. Your core will be strengthened, and the dissenters will be left to choose between three options: stay in relative obscurity, leave and give up their influence, or change. I don't want anyone to be lost. I pray that they will all choose to change!

---

[11]Winston Churchill, The Gathering Storm, (Boston, MA, Houghton Mifflin Company: 1950), 250.
[12]Churchill, 263
[13]Churchill, 168

22 - Stay at the Top of Your Business

There is no autopilot mode in youth ministry. You can't just create a calendar, empower a team, and go on an extended vacation. You have to remain prayerful and actively involved with the group. You have to be at youth events, services, and classes. You have to keep two fingers on the pulse of your group and one finger in the wind, anticipating trends in culture. You have to stay on top of it. Too much lag-time in identifying and solving problems will result in lives being lost. Pay attention to changing environment.

Do what you have to do, within biblical parameters, to stay one step ahead of changes in the world. Whether it's using social media to stay connected, addressing modern challenges to truth, or teaching teens to remain accountable in a digital world, don't be left sporting the skinny-jeans of ministry into a polyester bell-bottom resurrection.

Be aware of the prevailing winds of temptation that your teens are facing. I don't mean that you should subject yourself to the same temptations. Taking in an inoculating dose of evil will not make you some kind of antibody to their struggle. Pay attention to the world around you. Listen to teens talk. Ask them questions. Read current news and modern religious literature. We are admonished to "watch" and "pray." A knowledge of the world, coupled with the passion of the holy, will give you a vision for young people.

Stay a step ahead of sin, know and preach God's holiness. Read works like, "The Cost of Discipleship," by Dietrich Bonhoeffer. When the time comes, be ready to answer pseudo-science's revision to failed Darwinian Evolution. Michael Behe's, "The Edge of Evolution," will inspire you with the true glory of God's creation. Don't be caught flat-footed by doctrinal confusion like *"Love Wins."* Authors like, Francis Chan, David Bernard, and Talmadge French will help you to build a biblical framework to deal with fallacy.

A generation of leaders was taken aback by the Internet. They didn't prepare students to deal with this new temptation. Suddenly Christian teenagers across the world had instant access to pornography. We should have seen that coming. Even a cursory review of the world wide web should have jolted us into action. Identify what new trends in media and what technological advancements are posing hidden threats to our students' hearts and minds.

Pay Attention To Your Students

Get to know each student in your group. What are their hobbies? How are they doing in school? Who are they dating? What are they involved with? Where do they work? Do they have their driver's license? What kind of relationship do they have with their parents? Can you answer most of these questions for a majority of your students? If you can't, you've got some homework.

Basic information about my students gives me a platform to interact with them on a daily basis. "How was your game this weekend?" "How is your mom feeling?" "How did your SAT go yesterday?"

Are they faithful to church? Are they coming to youth events? Are they praying and reading their Bibles? What impression do you get from their actions at church? Do they engage in worship? Do they connect to the preached Word? Do they respond to altar calls?

I want to know how to pray for each student. I want to know how to best influence their lives through programs and leadership. I want to have a sense of when they need scolded and rebuked or encouraged and uplifted.

Are they struggling with lust? Is there a dating culture that needs to be monitored? Are they in to television and movies? Are they social media junkies? Are they struggling with depression? Are they estranged from a parent? Is anger a temptation?

Although I know in January what I'll be teaching in December, my knowledge of our student's needs gives me impetus to teach with urgency and passion. I recognize every opportunity to teach or preach as perhaps the last chance I'll get to bring them back from the brink, or help bring them into the kingdom.

Meet The Needs With Events

Is your group struggling with unity? Build events that create group togetherness. Friday nights are a critical element we'll discuss more in later chapters. Help them to form common ground through shared experiences.

Scare Them Into Each Others Arms

I don't particularly like Halloween. However, our group has a tradition that we revisit about every six years. Six years is how long it takes for everybody to graduate or forget the last time we pulled off this stunt. The boys get the girls into the woods in some way or another and scare them half to death. This past year we used the ruse of a scavenger hunt. First we got the van stuck. Then it got too dark to see. The girls didn't have flashlights. The leaders pretended to be lost. Then I "fell" and got stabbed in the stomach by a protruding root. Blood was pouring out of my shirt. In the dark it was particularly awful looking. About the time I was trying not to bleed to death, the boys started playing their part, as dark ominous figures drifting in and out of view. I have to admit, if I hadn't been a part of it, I would have been scared too. I knew we had gone to far when the girls started praying. I mean they were really praying, with tears. By the time the boys came out of hiding, the girls were so angry they wouldn't speak to us. Like I said, I don't like Halloween, and I don't believe in creating fear, but events like the one I just described create memories that everyone who was there will never forget. They have great value, even if it isn't immediately apparent.

Get them working together against an enemy. John Stuart Mill, in "On Liberty," suggests that external opponents create internal cohesion. Identify forces working against the group (i.e. poverty, witchcraft, abortion, addictions) and inspire students to fight together for what is right. They could have prayer walks, a time of fasting, Bible Study groups, or sacrificial giving.

Are students feeling listless or useless? Create a youth service where they minister to each other and to guests. Start a band. Are they struggling with materialism? Take them on a missions trip, or engage them in local outreach. Are students too caught up in pop culture? Create a Bible reading program. Award students that commit to reading their Bibles and praying.

I'm not suggesting that we overreact, or even that we act on every bit of information, or on each spiritual whim we get. We just shouldn't be the last to know that our ship is taking on water. We certainly don't want to be sitting at the helm of a boat on the bottom of the ocean trying to figure out what went wrong. Be prayerful. Be diligent. Be watchful. Don't be taken off guard.

When you identify a spiritual need or a dangerous enemy, act. Don't wait until next Sunday or next month. Don't put it off until that upcoming youth rally. "… if the watchman see the sword come, and blow not the trumpet, and the people be not warned; if the sword come, and take any person from among them, he is taken away in his iniquity; but his blood will I require at the watchman's hand" (Ezekiel 33:6).

However, when you feel the need to establish a new program that is more than just a single event, proceed with care. Students can be disillusioned by fits and starts. If you say you're going to have a monthly youth service, have it every month on the week you predetermined. If you say you're going to have a youth trip, make sure it happens. If you announce you're going to reward people who read through their Bibles, reward them. Don't leave them hanging in bewilderment because of knee-jerk reactions and inconsistency. I think Ecclesiastes 5:2 states it well, "Be not rash with thy mouth, and let not thine heart be hasty to utter any thing before God: for God is in heaven, and thou upon earth: therefore let thy words be few."

23 - Fight for Their Lives

I was six years old when I saw porn for the first time. Thirty-three years later I can tell you where it happened, the weather conditions that day, and exactly what I saw. I don't have a photographic memory. I couldn't tell you what I wore to work yesterday. But, an image I saw for a brief second, in the first grade, is forever seared into my memory.

I'm afraid that we adults have forgotten the power of sexual situations and explicit images. Our parents would never have engaged in sex on the couch in front of us. If we had peaked into the neighbor's bedroom we would have been called peeping toms and threatened with jail time. Growing up in the eighties, the only access we had to porn was the underwear section of the J. C. Penney catalogue, which my mom always destroyed—bless my momma. However, today, in thousands of Christian homes, children and developing teens have access to porn twenty-four hours a day, for free, and with impunity. They have cable TV in their bedrooms. They lay in bed at night with tablets and cell phones, they browse the Internet at home, alone. I've heard parents say that they trust their kids. That statement tells me one of two things. Either they are incredibly stupid, or they are too lazy to care.

A mother came to my wife and me with tears in her eyes because her thirteen-year-old boy had accessed porn on her computer.

I was incredulous when she expressed her total shock that he would do such a thing. I would have been shocked if he hadn't. Teen boy, left alone, access to the Internet... The end of that story will almost always be, "and then he looked at porn." Here is a wakeup call to every adult who has forgotten what it felt like to be nine, eleven, or fifteen: if a child is alive, he or she is in some stage of sexual development. As much as that is an awful reality, an even more poignant truth is that exposure to pornographic images will speed up the process. When I say pornographic images, I mean People Magazine, Vogue, Victoria's Secrets, erectile dysfunction commercials, Axe commercials, MTV, the iTunes homepage, YouTube's homepage, almost every Google image result—no matter what you're looking for and every single one of the millions of porn sites available online for free. Every time a child is subjected to these pornographic images the fire inside them grows more intense. God have mercy on them.

Some of the "stupid" people think that sexual exposure is harmless or maybe even positive. "Maybe a few sexual images will just get them pointed in the right direction," they might say. "At least they like girls," says the redneck, that is, until he finds gay porn his son looked at on his desktop. Then he wants to drag junior out to the cow pasture to teach him how to be a man. The adult is the one who should have been dragged out to a cow pasture to be taught how to be a dad. Every young man and woman has the power to choose whether to live for God or not. However, stupidity can contribute to bad decisions. Contrary to popular myth, there's no "gay gene." The statement, "I always knew there was something wrong with that boy," is about as stupid as drinking and hunting. Young people aren't born gay, they become gay. Two of the most powerful influences are "experience" and "exposure." A perfectly normal child who experiences rejection, negligence, or abuse may seek affection in a way that leads to aberrant behavior. Similarly, a child well on its way to a healthy heterosexual life, who has not had predisposing negative "experiences," can be knocked completely off course by what they see.

You could call porn, "rape of the mind." And this kind of assault is far more prevalent and nearly as damaging as rape itself. But, I fear that parents aren't seeing it that way. A father that would murder a man for raping his daughter "physically" will kiss her good-night and send her to her bedroom to watch HBO on her seventy-two inch flat screen. Behind closed doors she is as likely as not to watch any manner of sexual situation, from prostitution to bestiality. What is it that makes these two scenarios so different? With rape, pregnancy is certainly a fear. However, wouldn't the average father feel homicidal even if a man, or woman, simply fondled his daughter? Wouldn't we want that person thrown in jail? Why? What's the big deal? Did he break any of her bones? Did he shorten her life? Did he leave scars? Ah... scars. No, not physical, but mental scars. So, besides the threat of pregnancy, the damage done to the precious innocent girl is done to her mind. What is the difference between a feeling that happens through the sense of touch and the feeling that happens through the sense of sight and hearing? Perhaps there is a difference, but I think they are more similar than we think, and the threat is multiplied times more real.

I humbly submit to you, dear youth leader, that our teens are being raped over and over again by what they experience through media. They will not, they cannot, be normal. Before puberty has done its work, they have been forever robbed of innocence and the hope of happy marital intimacy.

Finally, there are parents who simply aren't aware that their child can access porn on a computer, tablet, or phone. First, these good folks should be stripped of all electronic devices. Then they should be taken out and beaten. Maybe that's too drastic. Another option; enter, youth pastor, stage right. It's our job to educate them about the danger, and start a fire that demands action. It's also our job to give them solutions.

Educating Parents

First, we have to educate parents. All the information you need can be found at: www.covenanteyes.com/pornstats/. Get parents—away from their teens—for a Wednesday night or Sunday morning. Make sure they understand the dangers of porn.

Next, teach them what to do about it. Here are some basic rules:

- Teens should never be left at home alone with access to television, especially cable channels like Showtime or HBO or Internet access.
- Teens should never be allowed to have private access to television or the Internet.
- Teens should never be allowed to have private access to cell phones, tablets, or laptops with access to the Internet.
- All devices should have accountability software installed. I recommend Covenant Eyes.

Covenant Eyes has simple instructions on how to install software on Apple products, Android devices, and computers.

Note: there are some additional actions necessary to make Covenant Eyes efficient on an iPhone or iPad.

1 - Go to "Settings"

2 - Click on "General"

3 - Click on "Restrictions"

4 - Click on "Enable Restrictions"

5 - Enter a password that your teen will not figure out and you won't forget.

6 - Click to disable the following:

    Safari

    Installing Apps

    Deleting Apps

    (button will turn from green to grey)

7 - Set ratings for Music and Movies

Now follow the instructions in Covenant Eyes to install and use the Covenant Eyes App.

Educating Students

At the same time we are trying to enlist parents to fight against the destructive power of media, we have to get into the fray. We have the leverage of dynamic youth ministry: youth events, youth rallies, chances to meet people around the district and the world, Youth Conventions, the opportunity to be a part of ministry, the presence of God, and relationship. Because we're with them consistently, we love them, and we're on their side, we can influence them.

Preach accountability. "I will set no wicked thing before mine eyes: I hate the work of them that turn aside; it shall not cleave to me" (Psalm 101:3). "But every man is tempted, when he is drawn away of his own lust, and enticed" (James 1:14). I teach that having a device that has the ability to access porn with no accountability is tantamount to sin. It's like having a stack of dirty magazines under your bed or a joint in your ashtray. It's wrong! The reality is this: A device with unrestricted access to porn will, with few exceptions, eventually be used to access porn. Don't engage in an uncertain battle in the middle of the night, alone in your bedroom. Draw the battle lines now, and attack the enemy here, in the safety of the day, while the Holy Ghost is speaking. Encourage teens to restrict their devices that day.

You can get even more aggressive with teens that are a part of any kind of ministry. Give them a speech, but don't wait for them to do the right thing. Make their involvement contingent upon accountability. If you love them, most will allow you to take this authority. Don't feel bad, you are saving their lives and your youth group. The last thing they need is a porn addiction, and the last thing you need is a ministry team manned by porn addicts.

Teach them about the destructiveness of perversion. If they don't take a stand for what Scripture declares to be holy, their lives will be swept away in a tide of sin and suffering. Sexual sin will steal their purity, peace, relationships, salvation, and ministry. Don't mince words. Two decades ago the sin of homosexuality was almost foreign to the Apostolic world I lived in. Today, it is everywhere. Politicians, athletes, entertainers, and educators have made it a daily discussion. Twenty years ago, what we associated with Sodom and Gomorrah, now possesses protected status. Decent people are losing their "shame" and their "ability to blush." The current state of debauchery is not ground zero. We are in a moral slide that will get worse and worse. What is next? I think our young people need to be challenged to think in these terms. Associate what is currently accepted in pop-culture with what they still think of as despicable. Help them to understand that God views the sin that we have labeled as acceptable with disgust, just as we would view something like child abuse or bestiality. If we don't take a stand on God's word, where will we stand? If we don't draw a line in the sand here and now, what will our children face? If we don't ally ourselves with Him, on judgment day where will any of us stand?

24 - Put Your Plan into Writing and Action

Whether your group is made up of five or seventy-five students, it is vital that you establish your program, *get it on the calendar*, and *follow through*. The road to hell is paved with good intentions and "faith without works is dead." The best philosophies and even real personal spiritual commitments can be derailed by failure to execute.

Create Your Calendar

It's November. The New Year is weeks away. This is the perfect time to create your calendar. Lock yourself in your office, or hole-up at Starbucks, and hammer out the details. Create a plan for Sundays, Wednesdays, and Fridays. Establish where the events will be held, what transportation will be needed, what staff will be involved, and what the programs will entail. It may seem like this is detail overkill, but it's always better to plan ahead rather than to try to get these details together on the fly. Many of the particulars will change throughout the year. That's okay. It's easier to make changes from week to week than to create a program from scratch only days in advance. Plan ahead. I promise this will save you many headaches.

Complete a tentative calendar, with your youth staff assigned to various events throughout the year. Submit it to your staff and volunteers. Give them a few days to respond with any changes they need to make. If volunteers don't respond, proceed anyway. You can't wait for weeks. If, in the end, they are unable to do events they never agreed to, find a replacement or change the event.

Indicate on your calendar what buildings or classrooms will be used for each event. You can also include an estimate of the hours it will be in use. Make a note of any church vehicles that will be necessary and reserve them in advance.

Once your calendar is complete, submit it to the pastor or church office for approval. After final approval, publish your calendar to staff and students in paper form, then online. Get a copy to your church media department for weekly announcements. Students should also be reminded of events and program details at the beginning of each week. Use text, Facebook, Twitter, email, or whatever other free service you can find to get the word out. Also take time at every event to promote the events that are coming up. The greatest program in the world can be undermined by poor communication.

Don't Cancel Events

You've worked hard in preparation, so don't cancel now. You have created your calendar, coordinated with staff, and promoted extensively, it is an absolute shame to cancel any event. Cancellation should be the very last resort. If you're sick, find someone to take care of the event. Call your aunt Bertha in a pinch… I'm not kidding. For me it's Aunt Sue. And every couple years or so when I call, her response is, "Are you kidding?" No, I'm not kidding. If there is a blizzard, change your event to sledding. If someone double-books the gym, go to the park, McDonald's, or *your* house. Pardon my melodrama, but I can't get the image of a broken-hearted seven-year-old boy out of my mind. He's wearing his Cincinnati Reds baseball cap and a little mitt. He's waiting at the front door for a dad that is not going to show up, again. These kids have plenty of people in their lives to let them down. I don't intend to join the parade. Hell and/or high water and all, we're having a youth event! They may not be able to count on much in their little lives, but at least they have this. The doors will be open. We will be there. We will smile at them. We will listen to their stories. We will care.

Out of money? Out of creativity? Out of ideas? Out of passion? The only truly indispensable part of a youth event is your time and love. Love costs you no money and is priceless to them.

Section Three
Programs, Classes, and Services

In the following chapters we will discuss Sunday classes, Wednesday Cell Groups, and Friday night youth events. I will only discuss a few of our event ideas. There are many other great ideas available. Read books, get online resources, and find out what other leaders are doing. Don't be afraid to be a copycat. There are no extra points for originality unless you're writing a book. Picasso said, "Good artists copy, great artists steal."

25 - Sunday Classes

Over the years we've experimented with three primary concepts for Sunday youth classes. We've tried different methods to address the following issues; the age of the youth pastor/teacher, ages of the people in the group, percent of teens actually attending class regularly, and problems and/or potential within the group.

Entertaining Teaching

As a young youth pastor I was struggling to get kids to attend our class. The group hadn't bought-in to our program yet. I didn't have the influence to compel kids to come. I was very frustrated.

We decided to develop lessons that were half entertainment and half inspiration. First, we found illustrations that were easy to promote. Most of the ideas capitalized on me looking like an idiot in one way or another. One week I was, Steve Irwin, "The Crocodile Hunter." One week I was dressed in a sweat outfit stuffed with Samson muscles. Another time we had a live snake. I ended up in a barrel of mud in a suit one Sunday. We used lots and lots of physical illustrations that were intended to feed curiosity and be entertaining.

Second, we made low budget videos and showed them in class a week in advance. We also played our promo videos in the hallway of the church. We did everything we could to get the word out that something crazy was going to happen in the next Sunday class.

I highly recommend this type of class if you are a new youth pastor/leader, if you are trying to build attendance, or establish a cohesive group. Actually, we have recently come back to this style of teaching because two new and younger teachers have replaced me in our Sunday class.

Preaching

Within two years of working with our group I began to transition away from entertainment to more of a youth service/preaching style. You are able to truly preach to students more and more as you gain their respect through the process of becoming the leader. There is no set time frame on when this will happen. You should be able to sense what they will allow you to do. I believe that teenagers need and want preaching.

Expository Teaching

The third and most powerful teaching style for our weekly Bible class has been expository teaching. This is a form of preaching that expresses the meaning of a particular text or passage of Scripture. It explains what the Bible means by what it says.

The first step is to get students to read the Bible. Bible reading is a weapon with multiple payloads. If we can get teens to read the Bible every day, the battle is half-won! If they read their Bible they'll be taught the principles of prayer, fasting, giving, loving, holiness, sacrifice, forgiveness, and every other scriptural mandate, from Christ Himself. What I teach will just be a reminder of what they already know that Jesus said.

In January we introduce our Bible reading program for the year. For the last couple of years we have used apps like the Blue Letter Bible and the YouVersion Bible. We help each student to begin a reading program on a phone, tablet, or computer. We've used programs like the *Seven Day Chronological Bible in a Year* from Blue Letter and The *Discipleship Journal Reading Plan* from YouVersion.

We have read through the Bible in a year or just the Old Testament or The New Testament.

Whatever we do, we do it together. Everyone knows what the Bible reading is for each day. Whatever you choose to do, know this, teenagers can and will read the Bible if they are inspired.

Each Sunday we begin class by asking who has read their Bibles and we talk about the upcoming assignment. We teach in an expository style from the chapters that the youth are reading that week. This should be a powerful and passionate time of teaching. It should cover the topics in the passages we've read. Don't duck hot topics and be careful not to ignore the text in favor of soap-boxing.

You can encourage teens to bring questions about the text or passages that meant something to them. It's easy, fun, and inspiring to give them a chance to share. Often I am in awe of their depth. These are true countercultural young people. They have no idea that it is absolutely abnormal for young people to read God's Word consistently, much less care about what they're reading.

At the beginning of class on Sunday, we ask each student, one at a time, if they did their Bible reading. If they did we give them some kind of candy, high-fives, or pats on the back. They understand that it is a priority. Consider establishing an annual incentive for those who have completed their Bible reading throughout the year. Incentives don't have to be lavish. Anything you do to reinforce Bible reading and studying will make a great difference in their lives. Over the years I have come to realize that my ideas won't get them to heaven. However, if we can get the Word of God in their hearts, they will never really be able to get away from it.

26 - Wednesday Night Cell Groups

The idea of Cell Group ministry is not new. It is loved, hated, and practiced in myriad ways. I was introduced to the idea through a small book by Paul Yonggi Cho, "Successful Home Cell Groups."

Several years ago our Wednesday night youth attendance was suffering. I was doing my best, but the students weren't inspired. After reading Cho's book I decided to implement our own brand of cell groups. Within months our Wednesday night attendance doubled, becoming our largest event of the week. It is easily one of the most successful things we've ever done.

Here Is How We Did It

We separated our youth into groups of approximately five students. For each group there was a leader, an apprentice to the leader, and the members.

We met with the leaders every Wednesday before service. We talked about rules, went over lessons, discussed goals, and assessed progress.

The leaders and the apprentices were responsible for leading their group, teaching the lesson, leading in prayer, and inspiring the members to participate and invite friends to join in. You can purchase curriculum or create your own. We did it both ways.

The goal was for each group to grow to ten members. At that point, the group would split, the apprentice would become the leader of the new group, and a new apprentice would be appointed for the two groups.

Our groups grew and multiplied quickly. Cell groups are wonderful evangelism tools, and they create an opportunity for our students to minister.

A Place For Cell Groups

The only place we had that was large enough to accommodate all our students was the gymnasium. This left the problem of how to create separate spaces for each group. What we did cost about three-hundred dollars and took an afternoon to build. We made a frame out of PVC pipe purchased from a local hardware store. Do a Google search for "PVC room divider." We made curtains to hang on our frame and, voilà, we had multiple rooms.

It was cheap, easy, and also portable. At the same time, our youth staff was able to monitor the groups without actually being in the room. Sometimes noise was a factor. However, it was not insurmountable.

27 - Friday Night Youth Events

For our youth team, Friday Night Youth Events are as important as anything we do. I don't mean to say that hide-and-go-seek and water-balloon-fights are as valuable as worship and preaching. We *have* a youth group to preach to and lead in worship *because* we have youth events. This is the primary time during the week that our students see us "living" and not just preaching. It's also the time when we can truly listen to them.

Our youth events typically start at six PM and last four to six hours. That is four to six hours of laughing, leading, loving, and listening. If we have time to listen, sometimes they will talk. Sometimes what they say will make us laugh, and often it will make us cry.

Actual Quotes From Some Of Our Youth

"I'm more interested in having quantity than having a lot of stuff"—that is an actual quote from a sixteen-year-old girl in our youth group. That one still makes me laugh.

What is the opposite of white? "Brown"—another actual quote… same girl.

"Dad got arrested again this weekend."

"Mom couldn't make it to my game last night because she's getting married."

Friday nights are not babysitting events. They are worth your time, energy, and money. If you will build great youth events, kids will come. If they are there, you have the power to influence them. Recognize Fridays for the tremendous potential they have.

You don't need twenty-five people to have a great youth event. If anybody shows up, your event has the potential to change his or her life forever. Don't lament the ones who didn't show. Capitalize on who did. You have just a few hours to make an impact and be impacted. Build an environment where they lose their inhibitions, forget their troubles, and embrace the life God has for them. We're like a good parent who figures out a way to get a child to take necessary medication. The one thing in this world that they really need is Jesus. We have to deliver the infinite God to limited teens in palatable proportions. "A spoonful of sugar..."

Youth Events Should Be Doable And Accessible

You can't make every event epic. You probably don't have eight hours every Friday to plan activities that can only be described in superlatives. It would be cool if you did, but more than likely, the effort to do so would result in burnout. They don't need "epic," they just need it to happen. I rarely ever spend more than a couple hours planning an event. A good average is probably thirty minutes. Make events simple and easy to pull off. Forget the overnight campout that requires ten chaperons, tents, sleeping bags, cooking utensils, waivers, and God Himself to pull it off. Try instead: crazy games in the gym that require a trip to Walmart, fifteen minutes at a computer, and a couple phone calls. The magic is not in the epic nature of the activity; it's in getting the group together, caring about them, and making it happen consistently. I also try to have consistent help planning and promoting events.

Make events accessible to teens. Most kids don't have the twenty-five dollars it's going to take to do go-carts, paintball, tubing, and other such events. At least they won't have it very often. Consider a middle to low-income family with three teens attending your event. At six dollars an event that's seventy-two dollars a month. This is approaching prohibitive for some families. If your events are too expensive, one of two things is going to happen: Either kids without money won't come, and you'll be the youth ministry reaching the rich. Or, they will come, and *you'll* be paying for them. I do have that t-shirt. Consider setting a reasonable cost—five to seven dollars—that remains the same for most youth events. This makes it easier for kids and families to plan. There will be times when even this reasonable price will leave you with extra money at the end of the event. Consider saving this money to offset the cost of a more expensive event.

In the end, make sure kids know they are always welcome to events with or without money. Watch out for that student who has too much pride to come and let you pay for it. Call their bluff and do whatever you need to do to get them to events. Their soul is at stake.

Youth Events Should Be Exciting

There should be lots of laughing. Although you have to be "large and in-charge" you should rarely, if ever, be mad. Stay on top of your emotions. These events are not about *your* plan, game, or program. It's about the kids, and if they are having fun, you are having success!

I'm not going to give a lot of details about specific Friday night youth events. First, there's nothing new under the sun, and I probably stole most of my events from the Internet. Secondly, *you* can steal thousands of youth event ideas from the Internet for free.

Here are twelve of my favorite youth events:

1 - **Film Festival:** Separate students into two or more groups. Each group writes, films, and produces a five to seven minute movie. Everybody watches the movies and eats popcorn. You can use an iPad or iPhone and edit on the device or use a laptop. You'll need a couple kids with some tech savvy. You may be surprised by the quality or lack thereof.

2 - Hide and seek: Need I say more? Inside, outside, both. Learn how to play a new way from an online resource or make up your own.

3 - Volleyball & Cooking: Separate girls into volleyball teams. Girls play volleyball. Boys cook for the girls. You can purchase items ahead of time or take the boys to the grocery and let them buy what is needed.

4 - Fashion Show: Separate the group into teams of two. Take the group to Goodwill. Each group can spend up to ten dollars on one outfit. The outfit can be funny or nice. Take the group back to the church and put on a fashion show. One person on each team does a catwalk while the other person announces the outfit. Encourage teams to use music or any available theatrics.

5 - Elderly Visitation: Get a list of elderly and shut-ins in your church. If you don't have any shut-ins, you can coordinate with a local nursing home. Ask shut-ins if they would mind if the youth group visits them on a Friday night. Set a specific time. Make a schedule of shut-ins you will visit. Have the youth group put care packages together (slippers, candy, books, fruit, et cetera). Visit the shut-ins, sing to them, pray with them, and give them their care package.

6 - Basketball & Cooking: Same as volleyball and cooking, except the roles are reversed.

7 - Video Scavenger Hunt: There are dozens of ways to do this and there are many lists online. All you need is two cameras (smartphone or tablets are fine). They go all over town filming items from your list for points. Watch the videos and eat popcorn. The team with the most points wins.

8 – Biking: Everyone brings a bike. Start at your church and travel a pre-planned route (make sure it is safe). Or you can get a trailer and take the kids and their bikes to a bike path/trail.

9 - Great Water War: You need a property that has an open field, some trees, and access to water. Separate the group into two teams. Create a boundary between the teams in the middle of the field. Teams are not allowed to cross the boundary. Each team gets a water hose and a couple thousand balloons. Give each team thirty minutes to build a fort out of whatever recourses are available and fill balloons. Hang a t-shirt inside each fort. Give them about an hour and a half of throwing balloons at each other and at each other's forts. At the end of the time period wring out the t-shirt in each fort. The team with the least amount of water in their shirt wins.

10 - Overhaul of the Youth Room: This is a great event if you have a space at your church that your students can decorate. Have teens bring pictures (printed on regular paper - not photo paper) of their favorite moments at youth events. Use Mod Podge to paste pictures to the wall or to a board that you can hang on the wall. This is an event that you can repeat over the years. It's amazing to look back on all the pictures. If you can, it is fun to paint the walls, make murals, and write messages with paint markers.

11 - Shop-a-Thon: Take the group to a mall and let them shop. The student with a receipt for the best deal wins. Simple and fun.

12 - $50 Scavenger Hunt: Hide a bag with $50 in it somewhere in the building. Create clues that lead them to the next clue. You can have as many clues as you want. More clues and greater difficulty will make the event last longer. Make them write down each clue when they find it. If you don't, many of them will ignore the clues and just turn your building upside down searching. You can use Bible verses as clues to make it more interesting and difficult. It's funny to watch teenagers running all over the building with Bibles. Allow yourself a couple hours alone in the building to hide clues and the money.

Youth Events Should Be Fun

How do we make youth events fun? Strangely, the answer is, structure. Youth events should be planned down to the minute. Plan who is going to do what and when. You do NOT want to "wing it." Be prepared. Have reservations, equipment, vehicles, buildings, food plans, et cetera. A lack of planning leads to misery for you and the kids. Plan, plan, and plan some more. And when you have done all to plan, let the chaos begin. After you have spent fifteen minutes introducing the "amazing marshmallow game," and then the place goes wild with kids running everywhere throwing marshmallows at each other... let it go. I guess what we're looking for is structured chaos, not the most organized game of marshmallow-ball ever played. Organization comes first, then chaotic fun. If you try chaos first, it rarely ends up being fun.

Youth Events Should Be Safe

People have entrusted us with their pride and joy. We have to do whatever is necessary to ensure the physical and moral well being of every student. Don't take chances with people's lives. Don't create events that are life threatening. A youth pastor I know had a child die during an event that involved four-wheelers. Don't drive recklessly. Make sure a youth leader is trust-worthy before you allow them to get behind the wheel of a van filled with kids.

Just as importantly, don't allow students to be in morally compromising situations. Make, state, and enforce rules that limit threats.

Don't let members of the opposite sex sit together in a bus or van. If you're young, I don't need to explain that rule to you. If you are a little older, let me remind you that a tremendous amount of romance can happen in the back of a van.

Don't allow public displays of affection. Don't create opportunities for kids to sneak off. Don't allow members of the opposite sex to be in each other's hotel rooms.

Never promote an event that will call for girls and guys to dress immodestly or act inappropriately. I'm still in shock from the "Christian Beach Camp" advertisement I received in the mail the other day. That's right, Beach Camp for Christian teens. Well … at least they may be Christians *before* they go. Nationally recognized Christian bands and speakers are meeting around the country at popular beach spots to hold these events. I'm trying to wrap my head around this. Christian teens are going to spend weeks prior to camp tanning themselves and picking out just the right swimsuit. Guys and girls are going to meet at places like Myrtle Beach, frolic all day, ninety percent naked, and then come together to hear a band and a Christian communicator lead them closer to Christ? Has the Christian world lost its mind? Who is this ignorant of Scripture? Forget Scripture, who is this ignorant? By any standard other than twenty-first century Hollywood, a bikini is at best partial nudity. The last time I met any man on this planet, nudity promoted lust. Lust leads to sin… and fornication, pregnancy, and anything *other* than an atmosphere conducive to teens getting closer to God. Spiritual death is more likely to be the result. Beach Camp is a concept conceived in the willful ignorance of Scripture. Use Godly wisdom. Don't create an event that is going to promote the absolute opposite of everything you're trying to do. This is one area where we must not fail.

Your doable, accessible, fun, safe, and moral event will act as a delivery system. What cargo will you dispatch? Their defenses are down. They are laughing, happy, and susceptible to your influence. What will you infuse into their souls? Will it be a healthy realization that you'd rather be somewhere else? Will you leave them with a passion to win a game? Or will we transmit the truth: There is one God and His name is Jesus, worship is glorious and materialism is meaningless, love is king, forgiveness is capital, grace is our hope, holiness is beautiful, and joy, peace, patience, kindness, goodness, faithfulness, gentleness and self-control are the fruits of a life lived for God. Everything in that list is countercultural. If we deliver these themes with consistency, in time, our youth group will be countercultural as well.

Section Four
Final Remarks

28 - What to Expect through the Years

This chapter contains my opinions about what might happen in your youth ministry. My opinions are based upon my experiences and observations. Actual experiences may vary. I might come across as a bit cynical. I apologize for that. I'm not trying to discourage you. I think it's best to face life with the best information available.

Phase One - Zero To Twenty-Four Months

First, let's assume you aren't replacing a previous youth administration. God bless you for blazing a new trail. Every church needs a youth ministry. They need you even more if there are only a handful of teens. There are pros and cons of being the first guy. Don't be discouraged by the cons. Just be ready to deal with them. At the same time, take advantage of the pros.

The Cons
- No established budget - It may take you some time to convince the powers that be that youth ministry costs money.
- No established territory - There may be other established programs that have laid claim to the calendar, the vans, the kids, and the building. Change is painful but necessary. You will

have to spend a fair amount of time marking fire hydrants until the church recognizes the validity of your program.

- No structure - In a program vacuum, negative routines tend to develop (i.e. attending sports events, movie nights at so-and-so's house, kids may be unfaithful to classes, services, and events, kids may sit on the back row and not engage in services, et cetera).
- No mentored students - If this is the first generation of youth ministry, you will not have the benefit of students that you've mentored. This lack of leadership presents some challenges.

The Pros
- Pioneer status - You may very well be recognized as a trail-blazer. Students, church members, and staff may appreciate your willingness to do what has not been done. Use this capital to get funds and establish your territory.
- No shoes to fill - "Brother-Last-Youth-Pastor didn't do it this way." These are painful words that you won't have to hear if you're establishing a new program. You won't constantly be compared. You're blessed! So, do everything in your power to be the kind of person that they'll measure every other leader by for the next century.
- No traditions to follow - A lack of structure means more work for you, but you'll get to create the program you think is right, without regard for what has already been done. Do your homework, find out what works, and implement your program.
- No baggage - Sometimes the last guy leaves students jaded and disillusioned. Don't become "that guy." Use the clean slate you've been given to establish a program that demands leaders to step up.

Now lets talk about what youth ministry might be like if you're replacing a previous youth leader and/or team. How this plays out depends a great deal on if the previous administration was good or bad. Here are some possibilities if he/she was great.

You'll probably be compared to the last guy. Assume you'll come up short, and expect to be rejected by teens, at least temporarily. If the departing leader has moved away, gone into some other area of ministry, or retired, you might be treated as though it's your fault that this beloved leader is no more. It's like jumping into a swimming pool in April. I don't know what to tell you other than, "Keep swimming; it gets better." This may last for six months or it may last for two years. I think the cultural norm is for a youth pastor to stay for about a year and a half before moving on. Those people that don't last beyond the two-year mark are missing out. Be countercultural. Stick it out. The first two years will be the very worst. But, even these frigid days can be marvelous and meaningful for you and the group you're working with.

Expect to be resented and challenged by any youth staff that you inherit. Multiply this by the number of years they've been involved, or how much older than you they are. You're going to work yourself to death preparing for your inaugural encounter. You're going to be all optimism and faith. Walking into that first meeting may feel something like finding a pole in the dark with your head.

Prepare to be usurped. Some may work behind your back to undermine you, or just to build themselves up. Consider that they may have thought they were the crowned-prince. Or, they may think you are ignorant, incapable, too young, too old, too energetic, too laid back.... The truth is, you probably are. Don't be offended. Give them some time. Be bigger than they are. Treat them with the respect you'd like to be given, and give them a couple years to get on board. God is patient. We should be, too. God is in a multi-millennial campaign to win the world. Waiting a few months before quitting, or before starting the public executions of previous youth staff members, isn't going to thwart the plan of God. Patience is countercultural. Try exercising all the fruits of the Spirit before laying down the law.

If you are following a youth pastor that left a bad impression, your experience could be very different than the scenarios listed above. There may be a lingering cynicism that you'll have to overcome. I don't know much about that. I've been blessed to follow in the footsteps of some wonderful men and women of God in youth ministry.

The final word on the first two years of youth ministry is this: stick it out. Quitting before the two-year-mark is like abandoning the gold mine two feet shy of the mother lode. The next phase and beyond have been some of the best years of my life. I could never have imagined how exciting and rewarding working with teenagers could be.

Phase Two: Two To Seven Years

The older teens you inherited from a previous administration are gone. And, great as they may have been, you may be glad to see them go. This is the time when you get to see twelve year olds step up to the plate and become men and woman of God. You'll get to watch goofy boys, who haven't recovered from their baby-fat, become leaders of distinction. You'll get to hear them preach their first sermons and lead with passion. Awkward, scrawny girls will mature into beautiful examples of holiness. You will have a group of kids that have been reading their Bibles, praying, and being faithful for years. With each year it just keeps getting better. It is during this phase that you can see a counterculture emerge from a group of disjointed teens. This is a force that draws people in, protects its members, and gives the world leaders that will not leave the world the way they found it.

During these years you'll establish your own plan. You'll discover your gifts. You'll do much less proving yourself and much more mentoring. You'll also find out what parts of your plan don't work. You'll focus on some things and leave others behind. Don't be afraid to admit that your brilliant plan was a flop. Not everything we think of is from God.

You'll make mistakes. It's okay to make mistakes. Don't be too hard on yourself. However, make sure your mistakes don't fall into the category of immorality. God is merciful, but we reap what we sow. Prisons are full of people who are paying the consequences of their decisions. There are a handful of things that we absolutely cannot do.

There is another small list of things that we must do. Pray, fast, read your Bible, and be submitted to leadership. You can overcome sin. It's critical that we make these simple principles a part of our daily lives. If we do, these years will be extraordinary.

You may experience some questions from your "friends" after you've been a youth pastor for five years. "So... you're still a youth pastor? When are you going to pastor a church? What is your five-year plan?" It can get frustrating when you couple these questions with the fact that the guy you graduated from Bible College with has been pastoring for three years. Don't feel the pressure to "move on" from youth ministry. Don't move unless it's the will of God. And don't confuse God's will with your impatience. The more mature you are the more effective you will be. Don't buy into the myth that youth ministry is for guys in their twenties.

Phase Three: Beyond Seven Years

If you make it into this category you are truly in an elite club. There are kids graduating from your program that started with you at twelve years old. Every student in the youth program came in under your ministry. Your younger students are being mentored by students that you have taught for several years. These new students are entering into a counterculture that is dominated by prayer and God's Word. The work is much easier and more rewarding during these years.

Parents trust you. You don't have to explain every detail of your program. You have been responsible and safe through a generation of teens. The entire church has witnessed the success of your program. The one question parents have about youth events is, "Are you going to be there?" If the answer is yes they have no more questions. This is a wonderful place to be.

At the same time, I want to strongly caution you about the danger of this place. Because the pastor and parents do trust you, there is much less accountability. If you say something is a good idea, or safe, people trust that it is. They would never imagine that you might do something dangerous or immoral. The problem is you're still human. You are as human as you were when you were twenty.

At this juncture, you need to work to create accountability in your life. Don't assume that things are going to be okay because it's been okay for so long. You need to be as careful, or more careful, than you have ever been. You have the ability to do youth events alone. Don't do it. Keep other adults involved. There will be girls or guys in your group that you visited in the hospital when they were born. Just because you're old enough to be their parent or grandparent doesn't mean that you are. Don't let your guard down. The truth is, you may be at a greater risk of moral failure at this point in your life than you have ever been. Don't let the work you have done for so many years be tainted by failure or accusations.

At some point you will begin to see your students getting married, starting families, and entering ministry. Ministry isn't about keeping score, however, it feels amazing to know that you played a small part in their lives.

We have some amazing people on our youth ministry staff that started in our youth program at twelve years old. Nobody has to tell them the importance of spiritual disciplines. They eat, sleep, and breathe them. Few things bring me more pleasure than working with these people.

Let me finish this chapter by saying a few words about burnout. After fifteen years of youth ministry I have gone through two major periods that I thought were the end of my career with teens.

The first was the night when the original kids that came into our program at twelve years old graduated. We had spent over six years with these kids. We had poured our hearts into them. We were tired, and I didn't think we could do it again. However, that same night, some twelve year olds graduated from the Sunday School program into the youth group. That was the beginning of the most amazing six years of our lives. We had never seen anything like these kids. They were nothing like the group before them and there's never been anyone like them since. God blessed us to see some extraordinary years of blessing.

When the group I just described graduated, I thought it was all over for me. That was two years ago. Now, we have another group that is so wonderful I don't know how to explain it. They truly love God. They love God like I've never seen young people love.

They are faithful, passionate, honest, and godly. These countercultural young people are going to turn the world upside-down. My seventeen-year-old son is a part of this group. And to think, I could have missed this.

29 - In the Yoke with Christ

Bruce was seven years old when his mother started sending him to a church near their home in Herrin, Illinois. At the time, their community, in the southern part of the state, had a population under ten thousand. It was a Sunday School teacher that really got his attention at that young age. Years later he would reminisce, "I will never forget Sister Patsey. I believe she really loved us." She surprised the seven-year-old by showing up at his house where she found him sitting in the front yard playing with his toys. She had come to invite him to the church picnic. It made an impression that he would recall many years later. There was nothing especially promising about Bruce or his family. In fact, even at that young age, he was aware that his home and circumstances left much to be desired. Nor did he attend the picnic. However, that Sunday School teacher's love left an impression that Bruce would share forty-seven years later.

Today Bruce is the director of Global Missions for a notable church organization with over two million constituents outside North America. He helped found a revival in El Salvador that has reached hundreds of thousands of souls. His life and ministry has touched thousands of ministers and missionaries. There are few places on earth that have not been affected in some way by that boy sitting in the dirt playing with his trucks.

How many "Bruces" are waiting for your ministry? They are in communities around the country. They are ignored, undesirable, and unwanted. Their homes are chaotic. Promises have been broken. Their hearts are heavy. They are waiting on someone to love them. Don't despise the small things, the poorly clothed, and unkempt ones. They are the very people for whom Christ died.

If you are currently unattached, and considering youth ministry, dive in! Of course it's good to hear the voice of God. We all love to have burning bushes. However, in the meantime, grab a sickle and go to work on the youth-harvest that is all around you. You don't need God to reiterate the mandate about pure religion. It is "to visit the fatherless and widows in their affliction." Youth ministry is undefiled ministry. It isn't about money. It isn't about clout. It's often thankless and a sure way to guarantee you'll be bi-vocational. It's probably not going to be the rung in your ladder to greatness, getting you a fantastic church pastorate. Here's how the interview may go:

Church pastoral selection committee: "What is your prior experience?"

You: "I've been a youth pastor for ten years."

Church pastoral selection committee: "Don't call us. We'll call you."

You don't need to work your way to the top. God "... putteth down one, and setteth up another" (Psalm 75:7). If you'll love people and work with integrity God will put you exactly where He wants you.

Don't do youth ministry with one eye on your work and one eye scanning the horizon for something more lucrative. Invest your soul in the soil of teenage hearts. The dividends are incalculable.

I've seen dead churches brought back to life by a passionate youth group. Anointed students worship like seasoned saints did when they were new converts. Teens are hungry. They are pliable. They are inspiring.

It may be true that a church is one generation away from extinction in a local community. It's also true that a church is one passionate youth pastor away from the greatest revival it has ever seen.

Don't get sucked in to working in some big church just because the pay is right. There are dozens of others, probably just as capable as you, who are standing in line for that same position. Go somewhere that no one else wants to go. Go to some impossible urban area that has no youth ministry. Go to a remote rural area that is equally reprobate, just with a lot less potential. Find a small church that can't pay a youth pastor. Attach yourself to a pastor that knows how to pray and fast and love. Don't let finances or a demographics chart set your course. Just find some place where the people are in need. That could be where you are right now, or it could be the next community over, or the next county. You may not have to go far. Of course, if your burden leads you to a group of seventy-five, that is honorable as well. Large groups need God, too.

If you're already involved with youth ministry, fight like you've never fought before. We aren't fighting against flesh and blood. This is a spiritual endeavor. Trendy "talks" and sophistication aren't enough for this generation.

Allison was a first-time guest in our church a few weeks back. There's always a temptation to put a dignified foot forward with new people. That Sunday was no exception. As much as I wanted to have good church, I wanted to have cool church too. Sometimes that's just not possible. I was a little worried when Sister Jones started laying hands on our first timer. Two weeks later, I had a serious reality check when Allison contacted us begging that we rebuke Satan, and maybe even cast a spirit out of her.

Allison doesn't need cool church. She needs "the power of God unto salvation." The students you are ministering to are as diverse as their fingerprints. But on the inside they are all spiritual beings struggling against sin and Satan. It is a life and death battle with eternal consequences.

Set a course and prepare for the long haul. Along the way, if you're anything like me, you'll feel inadequate. It's okay to feel that way… it's the truth! Do your very best, and at the end of the day, if God doesn't work, not one good thing will come of all your labor. "But if it be of God…" nothing can stop the countercultural revolution.

Countercultural Youth Ministry

My mother once shared with me a vision God had given her. She saw two oxen in a yoke. The first was inordinately short and thin. Its hooves barely touched the ground as the other animal dragged its scraggly little legs along. The second ox was colossal and imposing. Its bulging muscles flexed impressively as he easily did the work of both animals. We are the little oxen in the yoke with God. He requires us to be in the yoke even though our greatest efforts will be so small. Pray, fast, study the Word, love the lost, preach, put together a program of classes and events, and "... having done all, to stand" (Ephesians 6:13). "... stand still, and see the salvation of the LORD" (Exodus 14:13). His glory, added to your effort, is enough to accomplish the task. God bless you as you labor with Him to see a group of ordinary students become countercultural.

June 7, 2016
Seymour, Indiana

www.ingramcontent.com/pod-product-compliance
Lightning Source LLC
LaVergne TN
LVHW051639080426
835511LV00016B/2394